THAMES VALLEY ILLUSTRATED WALKS

Trevor Yorke

COUNTRYSIDE BOOKS
NEWBURY, BERKSHIRE

COUNTRYSIDE BOOKS
3 Catherine Road
Newbury, Berkshire

To view our complete range of books,
please visit us at
www.countrysidebooks.co.uk

ISBN 1 85306 661 3

Designed by Graham Whiteman

Maps, photographs and illustrations
by the author

Cover pictures of Maidenhead and Wittenham Clumps
supplied by John Bethell

Produced through MRM Associates Ltd., Reading
Printed by J. W. Arrowsmith Ltd., Bristol

CONTENTS

Walk

Publisher's Note

We hope that you obtain considerable enjoyment from this book; great care has been taken in its preparation. Although at the time of publication all routes followed public rights of way or permitted paths, diversion orders can be made and permissions withdrawn.

We cannot of course be held responsible for such diversion orders and any inaccuracies in the text which result from these or any other changes to the routes nor any damage which might result from walkers trespassing on private property. We are anxious though that all details covering the walks are kept up to date and would therefore welcome information from readers which would be relevant to future editions.

INTRODUCTION

Maps are wonderful things. Just a few lines and symbols on a page and the shape of the landscape takes form. Draw a cross next to a wavy line and most people would expect to see a church by a river. We use them every day to find our way around town and country, and draw them ourselves when giving directions. We even hang antique maps on our walls as decoration. Yet despite all this familiarity, when it comes to walking books, they tend to take second place behind masses of monotonous and ambiguous text.

With these facts in mind and by calling on my experience in surveying and illustration I set out to produce a book which uses maps to guide you around the walk.

To ensure that you successfully negotiate the walks, I have used strip maps whereby you follow the walk up the page in the direction of the arrows. This permits a larger scale and therefore allows me to show small details on the ground which can make the difference between taking the correct route or not. Also by imposing some approximate contours and shading I have given the map a third dimension.

Another advantage of this format is the extra space that can be dedicated to explaining the features you see and illuminating them with stories and illustrations.

I am, like so many people, drawn to the Thames more than any other English river for perhaps two reasons. Firstly is its historical significance. The river passes through the capital city and therefore has attracted Parliament and Palace to its shores and, with them, all the associated men and women in positions of importance. Secondly and of more subtlety, is the countryside through which it flows. Gently rolling hills, capped with a seasonal patchwork of lime greens, golden yellows and copper reds, command spectacular vistas of its snaking silver body, while a short descent will lead you to the lush meadows and pasture through which winds the river, and its new faithful companion the Thames Path, permitting unrivalled access to this most exclusive of waterways.

Each walk starts from the nearest suitable parking spot to a selected pub, although the landlord may be happy, if asked, for you to use the adjoining car park. When parking, please be considerate to locals and avoid stopping directly outside houses or blocking driveways and farm gates. Despite not being a specialist pub walking book I have endeavoured to ensure that the main hostelry is of a good standard and some in my opinion are exceptional. Assume opening times are approximately 12 noon to 3pm and 7pm to 11pm with last orders for food usually at 2pm. (Some pubs do not serve food on Sunday evenings or on Mondays.)

Although the strip maps are easy to follow, you may wish to carry the relevant OS map. The OS Explorer maps 159, 160, 170, 171, 172 and 180 cover the area featured as do the Landranger series Nos 164, 174, 175 and 176.

With these walks you may discover places you never realised existed or perhaps you may look at familiar areas from a new perspective. Whichever is the case I am sure by the end you'll appreciate our good fortune at being able to enjoy the varied landscape reflected in the mighty waters of Old Father Thames.

Trevor Yorke

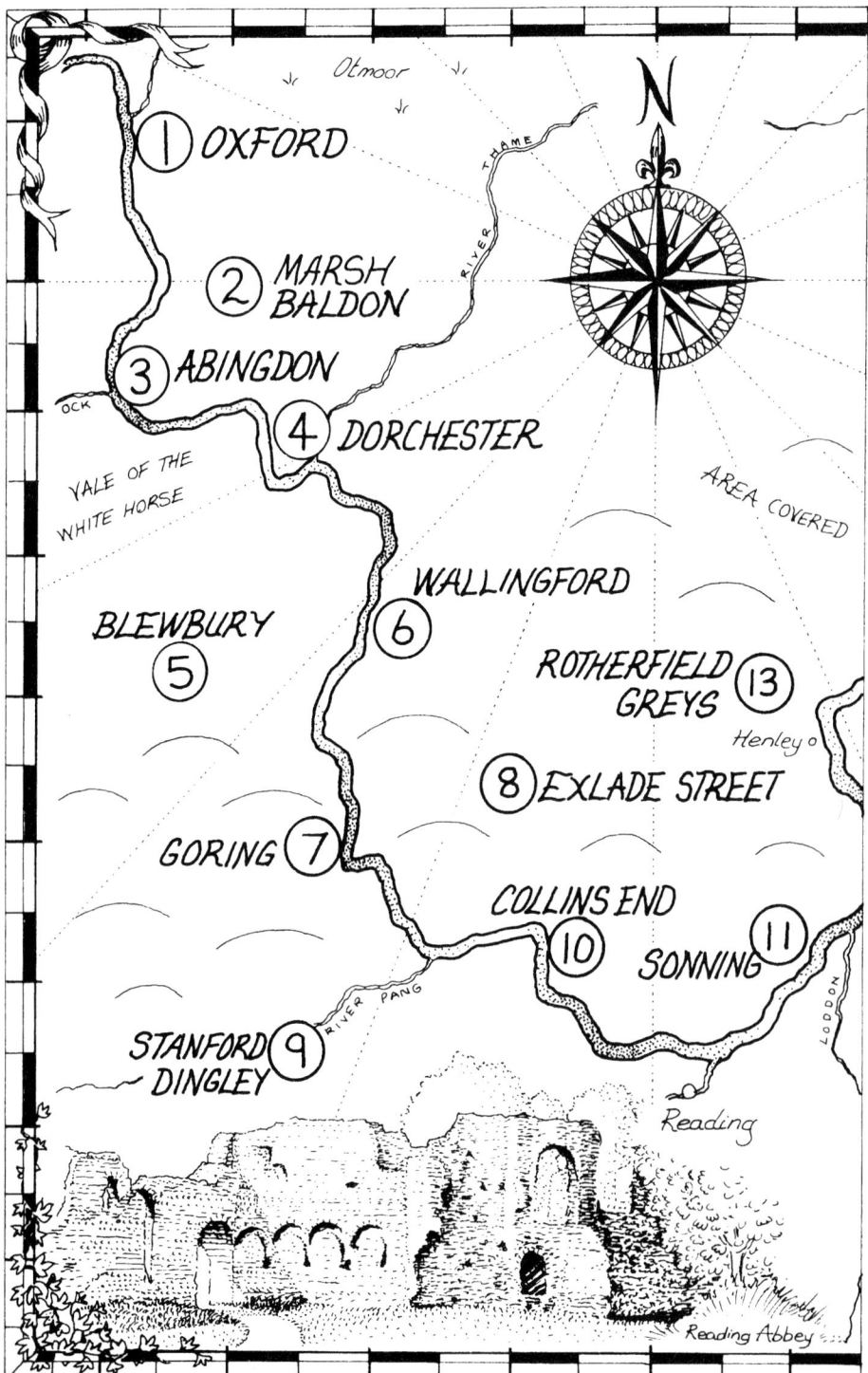

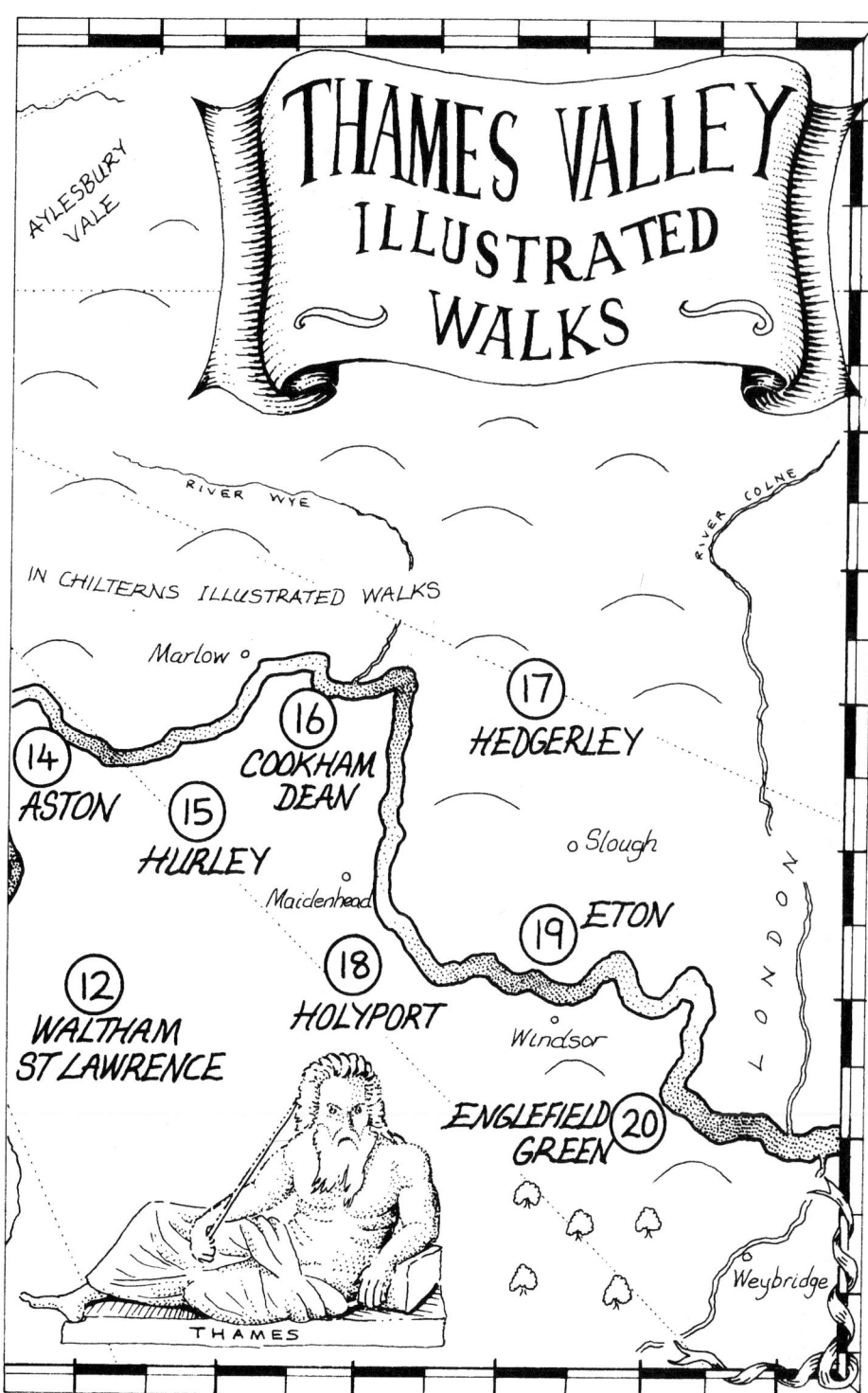

USING THE MAPS

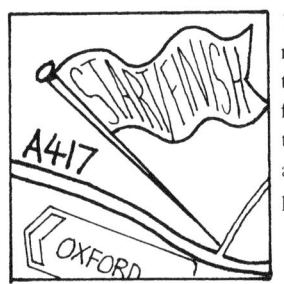

1. Using the area map and 'Getting There' text, find your way to the parking area and Start/Finish point.

2. Start walking in the direction of the arrows up to point 1 in the black circle.

3. Continue from point 1 on the next map. (The darker shaded areas are higher and the lighter areas are lower.)

4. The white arrows are parts of the walk covered on another map.

KEY

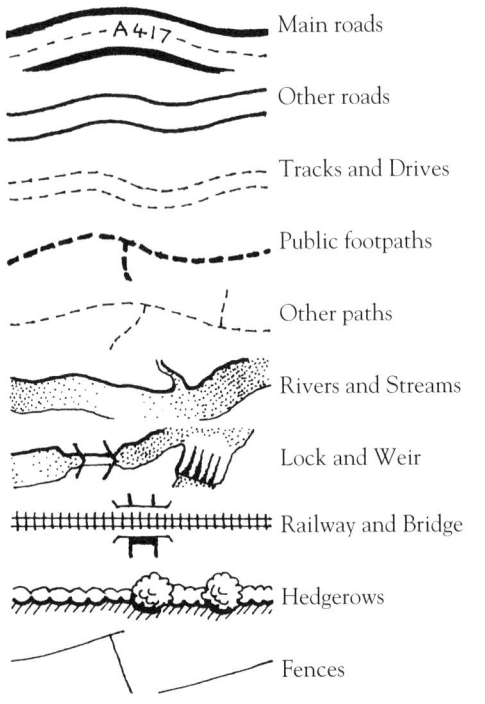

Main roads

Other roads

Tracks and Drives

Public footpaths

Other paths

Rivers and Streams

Lock and Weir

Railway and Bridge

Hedgerows

Fences

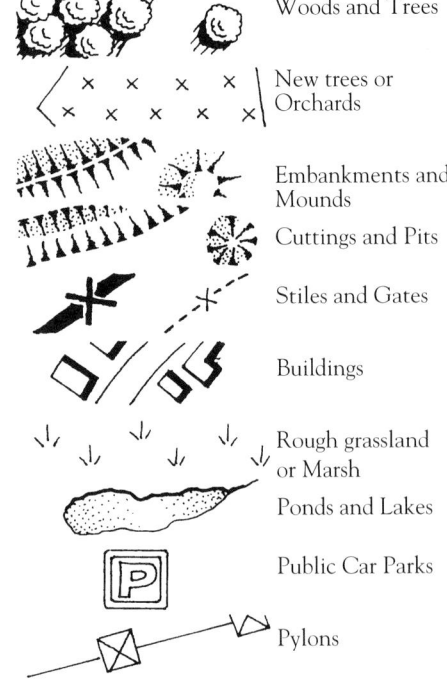

Woods and Trees

New trees or Orchards

Embankments and Mounds

Cuttings and Pits

Stiles and Gates

Buildings

Rough grassland or Marsh

Ponds and Lakes

Public Car Parks

Pylons

Walk 1
BINSEY AND OXFORD
Length 4½ miles

St Michael's and Cornmarket St.

GETTING THERE: Use the A34 from north or south and turn off at the A420, Botley Interchange, to head east towards the city centre. Just past the Halfords store turn left up Binsey Lane, and follow it for a mile to the village. Parking is limited to the road-side before the pub. Alternatively you can use the Seacourt Park and Ride which is just after you come off the A34. Catch a 400 bus to Carfax and start the walk there. The pick up point when you finish is in Castle Street.

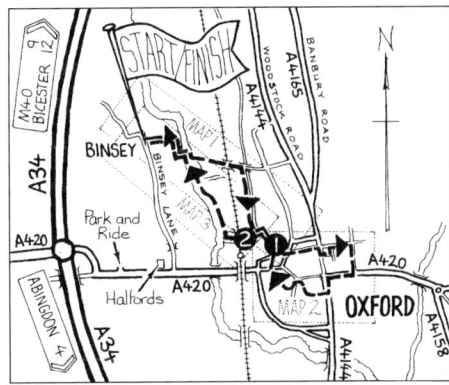

MOORING: There is mooring along the Thames near the Perch at Binsey.

TERRAIN: Flat and mainly well-made paths, but a few muddy spots.

START: (GR 492076) From your roadside

parking head towards the Perch but turn right through the gate and along the gravel track in the field before the pub.

INTRODUCTION: Few cities can have within a short walk of their centre an idyllic hamlet and pub set in isolated fields! The

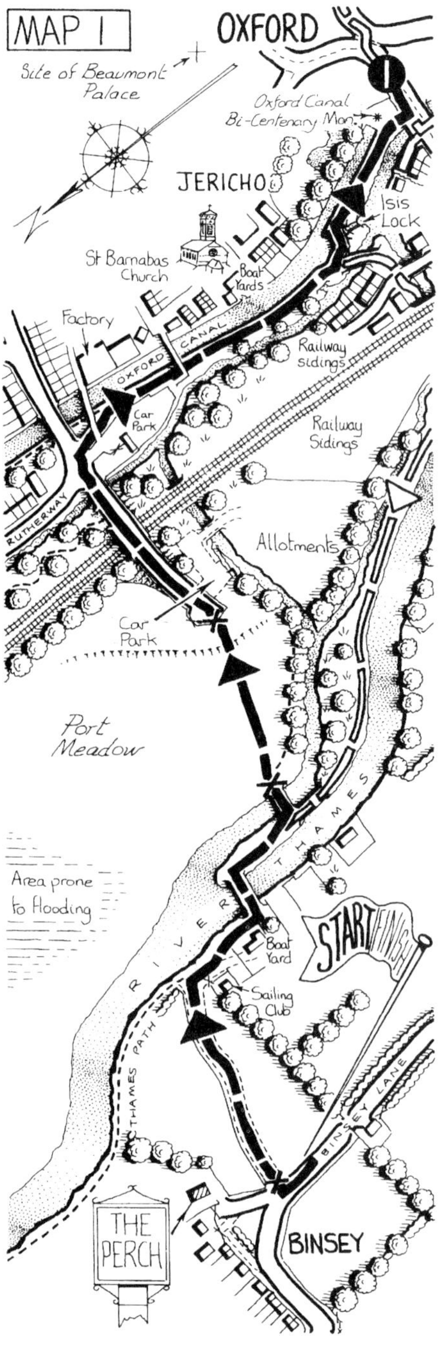

MAP 1

OXFORD

Site of Beaumont Palace

Oxford Canal Bi-Centenary Mon.

JERICHO

Isis Lock

St Barnabas Church

Boat Yards

Factory

OXFORD CANAL

Railway Sidings

Car Park

Railway Sidings

RUTHER...AY

Allotments

Car Park

Port Meadow

Area prone to flooding

RIVER THAMES

THAMES PATH

Boat Yard

START/FINISH

Sailing Club

BINSEY LANE

THE PERCH

BINSEY

tranquillity of Binsey is in marked contrast to the chattering masses milling around the masterpieces of Oxford less than two miles away! You could fill a library with all the books that have been written about this square mile of architecture, so in this journey I have concentrated more on 'Town' than 'Gown'. There is an ancient meadow, a canalside walk, castle remains, a Saxon tower but still time for the obligatory tour of Oxford's academic heart.

ST BARNABAS' CHURCH: This commanding Italianate edifice looming over the canalside boatyards was designed by Arthur Blomfield in 1869. His brief was that it should be solid and devoid of external decoration (cheap in other words!), so he used rubble and cement with only horizontal bands of brick to break the monotony.

The church was also used in Thomas Hardy's *Jude the Obscure*.

St Barnabas' church.

PORT MEADOW: When an American tourist asked a local professor to show him the most ancient place in the city, he was surprised to be taken to Port Meadow. The first known settlements in the area were here, back in the Iron Age, a thousand years before Oxford was established. In the 17th and 18th centuries this was the site of the Duke of Marlborough's Racecourse, the route of which can still be traced. One of the first ever powered aircraft crashed at the north end of the meadow and it was still being used as an airfield in the First World War.

THE OXFORD CANAL: It was completed in 1790 primarily to bring coal from Warwickshire to the city. The old wharf where this was unloaded is now lost under the car park on the south side of Hythe Bridge Street with the truncated arm now used for residential moorings.

OXFORD: Described by Jude as 'the Heavenly Jerusalem', this romanticised city of architectural splendour has originally more in common with Milton Keynes than its great rival Cambridge! Whereas the latter has pre Roman origins, Oxford was first established as a Saxon planned town in around AD 900. It was one of the line of 'burhs' like Wallingford (see Walk 6) and had a grid layout of straight roads which still exist today (the east end of the High Street which curves was not in this original grid). Oxford's position at the junction of three kingdoms made it an important meeting and trading centre and in less than two hundred years it had become the second largest town in England.

A downturn in commercial fortune with the arrival of the Normans was somewhat rectified with the establishment of numerous monastic houses in the 12th century

St George's Tower

making the town a centre for learning and debate. When in 1167 Henry II banned students from studying in Paris, Oxford became their obvious choice and by 1221 the first Chancellor of the University had been appointed. There were no colleges at this point only academic halls, which were typically narrow houses run by a graduate with a hall and accommodation on the upper floors and a shop leased out below. Conflict between Oxford's older commercial side and the new academics culminated in violence in 1355 when townspeople ran riot for three days killing six clerks and sacking halls. As penance for this the Mayor and Burgesses had to attend a humiliating ceremony on every anniversary until 1825!

More importantly, the power gained afterwards by the embryonic colleges, along with the abandonment of land after the Black Death, enabled them to rapidly expand. Despite this boom time most of the college buildings which form Oxford University today date from the 17th and 18th

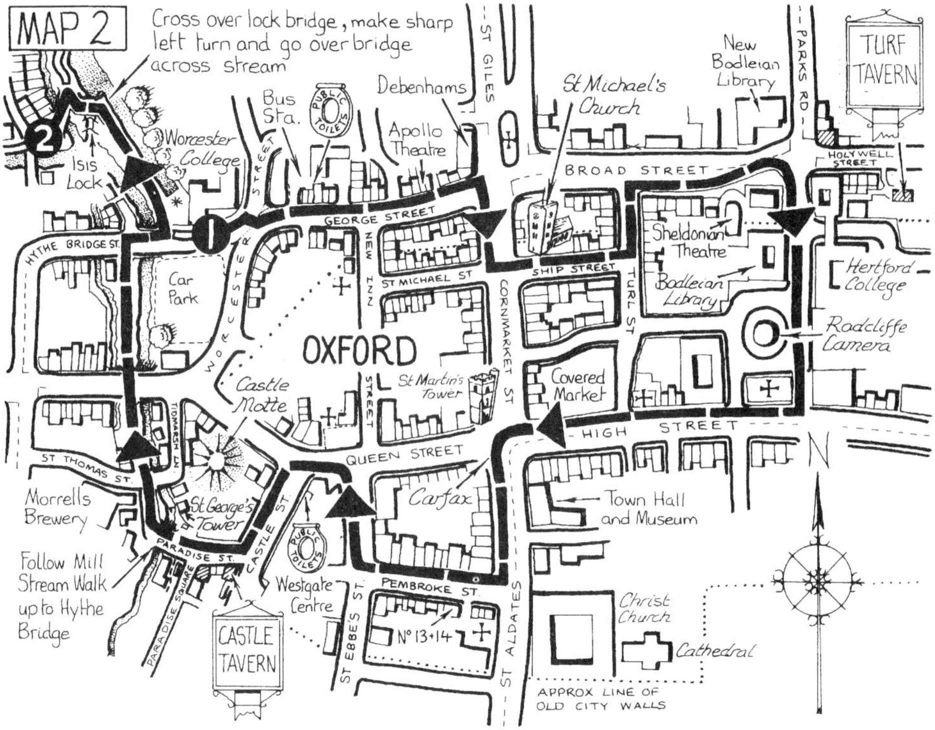

MAP 2

Cross over lock bridge, make sharp left turn and go over bridge across stream

Bus Sta.

Debenhams

St Giles

St Michael's Church

New Bodleian Library

Parks Rd

TURF TAVERN

Worcester College

Apollo Theatre

BROAD STREET

HOLYWELL STREET

2

Isis Lock

GEORGE STREET

Sheldonian Theatre

Bodleian Library

Hertford College

Radcliffe Camera

HYTHE BRIDGE ST

Car Park

NEW INN HALL

ST MICHAEL ST

SHIP STREET

CORNMARKET ST

TURL ST

OXFORD

Castle Motte

St Martin's Tower

Covered Market

HIGH STREET

N

ST THOMAS ST

QUEEN STREET

Carfax

Town Hall and Museum

Morrell's Brewery

St George's Tower

PARADISE ST

NEW ROAD

CASTLE ST

BONN SQ

PEMBROKE ST

Christ Church

Follow Mill Stream Walk up to Hythe Bridge

Westgate Centre

ST EBBE'S ST

Nº 13·14

ST ALDATES

Cathedral

CASTLE TAVERN

APPROX LINE OF OLD CITY WALLS

centuries when student numbers were actually in decline.

BEAUMONT PALACE: This royal residence was the birthplace of Richard the Lionheart and possibly his maligned brother John. It became a friary in 1256 but only exists now in the street name.

ST MICHAEL'S: The Saxon tower of this often overlooked edifice is the oldest structure still standing in Oxford. Originally it was a freestanding tower built into the early earth and timber ramparts of the then town's defences (see picture). In the 12th century a new church was built linked to the tower and the wall was diverted around the new building.

The Saxon town walls were replaced later that century by a massive stone one with 21 towers! If you get the chance to go

Conjectural view of St Michael's c.1080 (Compare with title picture).

up Holywell Street you can see a remaining stretch of this wall through the gateway to New College.

SHELDONIAN THEATRE: Christopher Wren's first major work was built between 1663 and 1669. The heads standing on the semi-circular wall in front are known as the Emperors but the present ones are fibreglass replacements!

The Radcliffe Camera, Oxford.

CATTE STREET: The richest hundred yards of architecture in the country face onto a street named after 'the mousecatchers'. Image conscious Victorians renamed it Catherine Street but it reverted to Catte Street in 1932.

RADCLIFFE CAMERA: This landmark building was designed by James Gibbs and finished in 1749 as an independent library. Only in 1862 did it become a reading room for the Bodleian Library and was renamed 'Camera' (Latin for 'Vaulted Room').

BODLEIAN LIBRARY: The main quadrangle beside Catte Street dates from 1624 and is notable for the Tower of Five Orders which you can view from within the quad looking east. They are from top to bottom: Composite, Corinthian, Ionic, Doric and Tuscan.

The New Bodleian Library is linked to the Old by an underground conveyor belt which hopefully functions better than its lock in which a silver key broke when King George VI performed the opening ceremony in 1946!

BRIDGE OF SIGHS: This famous bridge linking the two sides of Hertford College was only built as recently as 1914!

CARFAX: The name means 'four forked' and this was the original centre of the Saxon town where the four roads crossed. St Martin's Tower is all that remains of the church, the body of which stood alongside the HSBC bank and was demolished in 1896.

PEMBROKE STREET: A colourful and ancient row of houses including Nos 13-14 which when viewed from the rear betray their 17th century origins.

OXFORD CASTLE: The motte (mound on which the keep stood) was raised in 1071 but it probably was not until the mid 13th cen-

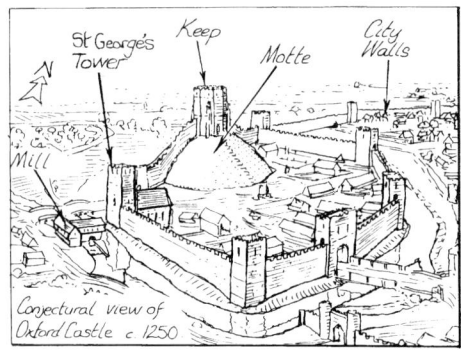

Conjectural view of
Oxford Castle c.1250

tury that the castle achieved its zenith (see illustration). It was virtually ruined by 1400 only to be repaired when the Royalists made it their headquarters during the Civil War.

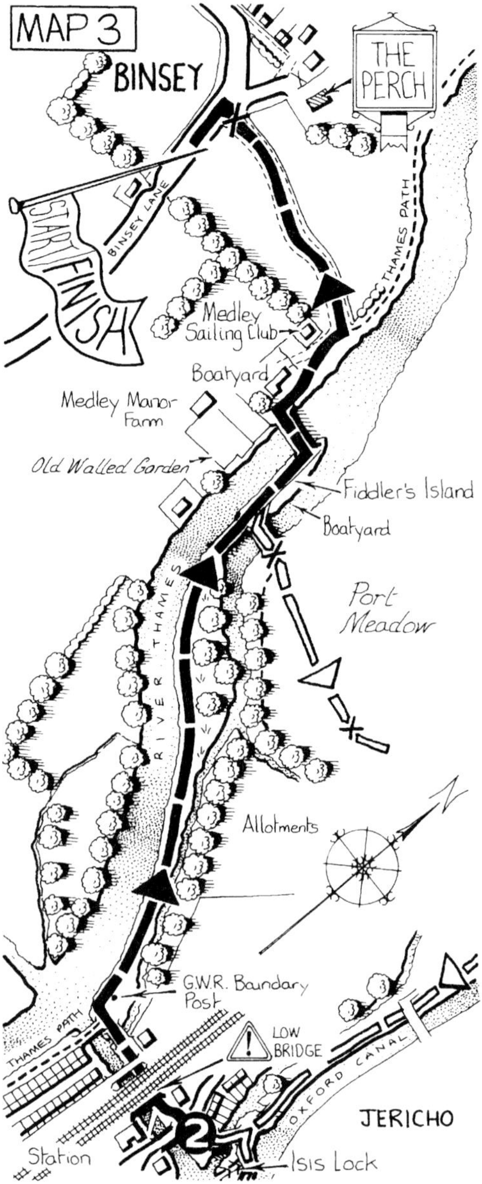

The townsfolk were reluctant hosts especially to the hated Governor Aston. He was only removed when while showing off to some ladies he was thrown from his horse and had to have a leg amputated! (He was ironically replaced by Colonel Legge.) Aston ended up in Ireland where he was beaten to death with his own wooden leg!

The castle was demolished after the Civil War with the only remaining building being St George's Tower which stands over the site of the old Castle Mill (see page 11).

BINSEY: A tiny hamlet blessed with an excellent pub. The blessed theme is appropriate as this was the route taken by pilgrims to the well at St Margaret's church (half a mile further up Binsey Lane). The waters according to legend were called forth by St Frideswide to restore the sight of a Saxon king who having taken a fancy to her discovered that 'Love is Blindness'! The Treacle Well featured in *Alice's Adventures* *in Wonderland* is in fact this one, although the 'treacle' part is actually the old word for 'cure' or 'healing fluid'.

REFRESHMENTS:

THE PERCH. Idyllic 17th century thatched building with huge and popular garden. Possibly on the site of an even earlier inn to serve the passing pilgrims. Telephone: 01865 240386.

THE TURF TAVERN. Popular because of its character and hidden position, it will make a good halfway house (or finish if you started your walk from Carfax). It was renamed in 1845 after the neighbouring gambling hall where 'turf' accountants met. Best access is from Bath Place which is a right turn just down Holywell Street. Telephone: 01865 243235.

There are also numerous places to eat in the town centre. If you want to pick up a snack then try the HEROES SANDWICH BAR in Ship Street which is even open on Sundays.

Walk 2
MARSH BALDON
Length 4½ miles

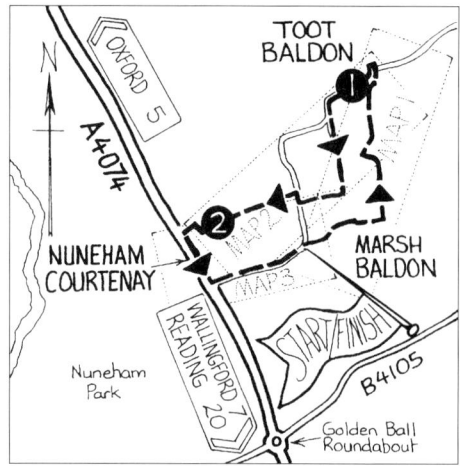

Toot Baldon

GETTING THERE: From the Oxford Bypass take the A4074 towards Reading and after passing through Nuneham Courtenay turn left to the Baldons. From Reading head north up the A4074, over the Golden Balls roundabout and then one mile further on take the right turn to the Baldons. This road leads you through the old gateway and up to The Green by the Seven Stars pub. Parking is probably best along the roads around The Green.

TERRAIN: Mainly flat with a few steep and muddy hollows.

START: (GR 562992) The walk starts from outside the Seven Stars and goes along the track on the southern end of The Green.

INTRODUCTION: Three picturesque villages standing along the ridge which overlooks Oxford are the corner points of this mean-

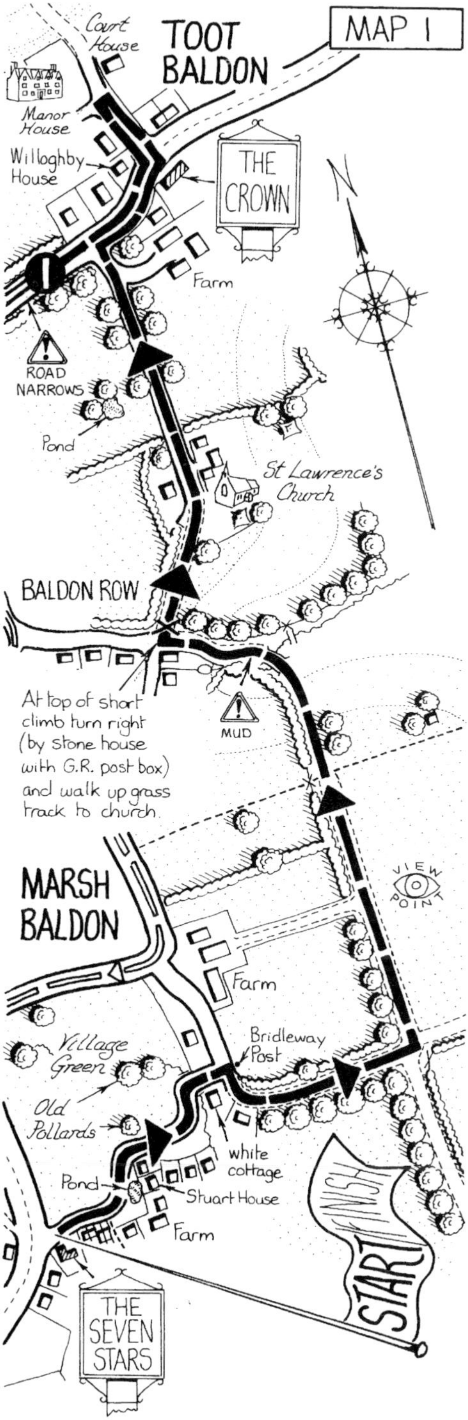

Map

MAP 1

Court House

TOOT BALDON

Manor House

Willoughby House

THE CROWN

N

Farm

⚠ ROAD NARROWS

Pond

St Lawrence's Church

BALDON ROW

At top of short climb turn right (by stone house with G.R. post box) and walk up grass track to church.

⚠ MUD

MARSH BALDON

VIEW POINT

Farm

Village Green

Bridleway Post

Old Pollards

white cottage

Pond

Stuart House

Farm

THE SEVEN STARS

START/FINISH

dering walk. Although they are unified in their attraction today their histories are notably different. One was protected by a college, another by a leading agriculturalist, both of whom resisted change to the structure of their villages, while the third was a completely new foundation by an 18th century landlord. In between, the relatively flat landscape is enhanced by some fine views and broken in places by hollows cut by streams escaping from the grassy plateau.

MARSH BALDON: Baldon is derived from 'Bealda's Hill' and the prefix presumably from the state of the ground, yet sometime in the past it was 'March Baldon' which implies a boundary. One feature which could have acted as this was the Roman road from Alchester (Bicester) to Dorchester (see Walk 4). Its course ran along the route you walk from New Farm, past Thurfield Cottage and up to the east side of The Green (Map 2).

The Green itself is probably the oldest part of the village visible today. All the villagers had rights to use it and there were strict annual dates for haymaking and grazing certain animals. Disputes inevitably arose, the most notable being in 1763 when a certain Yateman made a bridge onto the green for his carts to pass over it, only for the Lady of the Manor to block it with pales. She then had a trench dug to stop his carriages and when he put planks over it she had elms planted to further halt his progress!

Baldon Row

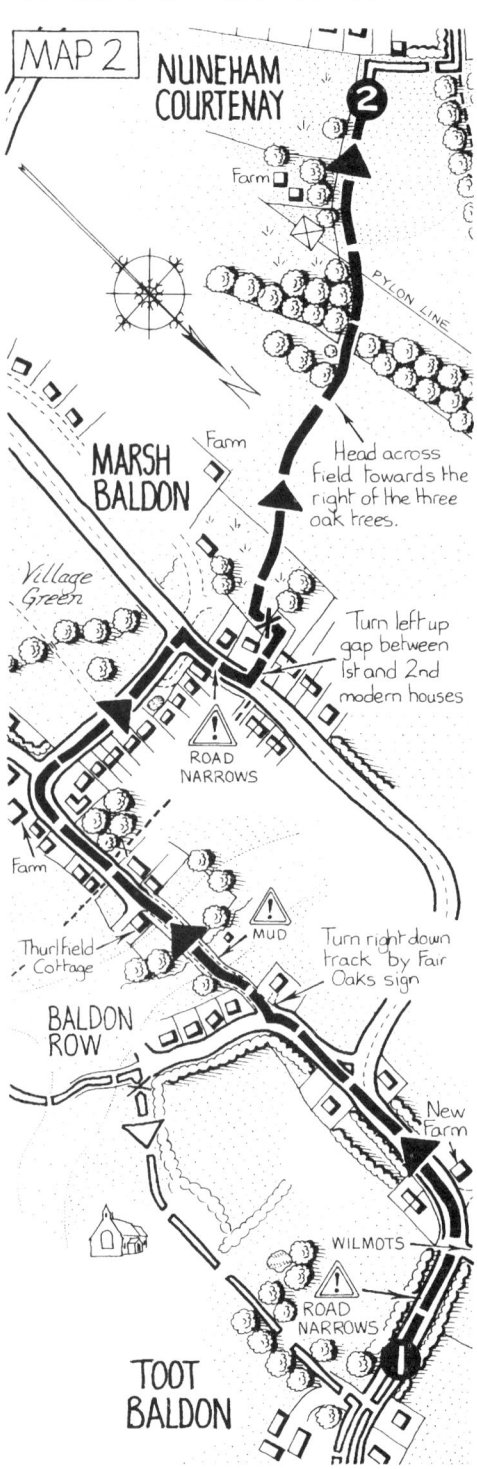

The Victorian cottages along the north side of The Green were built after a fire in 1866 which had blazed out of control as the then numerous ponds had dried up. Today there are only two ponds left and most of the trees have gone.

TOOT BALDON: 'Toot' means 'Look Out' and if you walk past the Manor House you can see why. Unfortunately what should be a stunning vista of Oxford's spires is blotted out by an electricity sub station and the Cowley car works! The Manor House is an impressive three-storey stone house dating back to the 17th century and along with the Court House and the Crown pub makes an attractive centrepiece to the village. In 1509 the Manor of Toot Baldon was given to Queen's College, Oxford, which enabled students to reside here at times of plague, which included the entire college population in 1519!

BALDON ROW: Now no more than an old school and a string of houses near St Lawrence's church, but it was probably the original Baldon village. The church has Norman origins but is visibly Victorian, like the vicarage of 1860 to the north of it.

NUNEHAM COURTENAY: Until 1760 the village stood to the west overlooking the Thames, but then Earl Harcourt decided to rebuild his house and moved the entire village out of view to the new site on the Oxford road. He built the identical sets of brick semis which neatly line the main road along with an inn, and blacksmith's (now the garage). There was little complaint from the villagers who had dry new houses, and the Rector only grumbled because he had to move his plants!

Harcourt built his new house and gardens called Nuneham Park on the old vil-

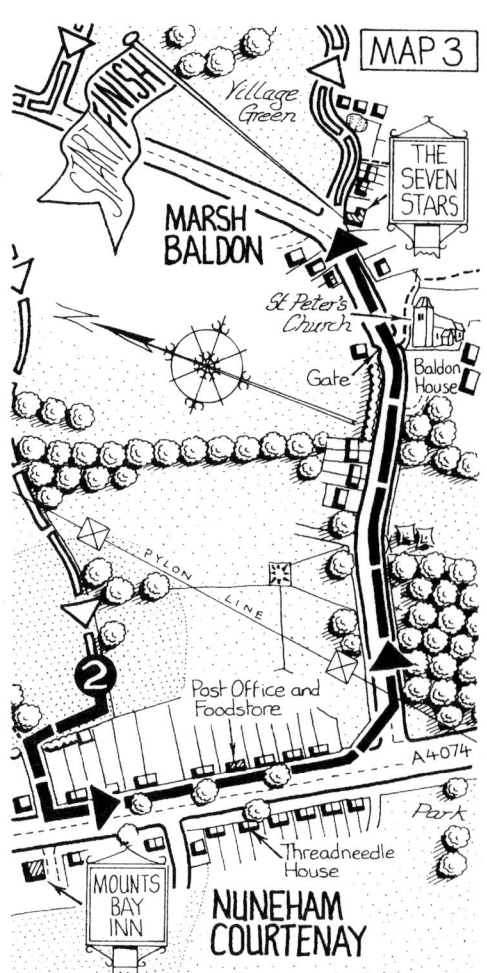

lage, believing that the view over Oxford would remind those with a Classical education of the view of Rome from the Campagna. One guest who seemed uninspired by this was William Buckland, a Professor of Geology, who had a reputation for eating every living thing! 'How does one know that something is unfit to eat until one has tried it,' he once said. Bearing this in mind his host should have thought twice about showing him the preserved heart of the King of France which Buckland promptly tried to consume!

ST PETER'S CHURCH: The most striking feature of this church is the tower which was constructed to take a spire that was never built! Also of note is an ancient sundial inside the porch above the south doorway.

BALDON HOUSE: A 17th century building hidden behind trees which has a folly made from parts of the old church at Nuneham Courtenay when it was removed in 1760. Baldon House's most notable owner was Sir Charles Willoughby, an innovative agriculturalist who supported the opening of the Oxford Canal to transport coal ash which he used as fertilizer! He also tried pigeon dung and strangest of all... rags!

REFRESHMENTS:

THE CROWN, Toot Baldon. Notable original village local with excellent food (best to book if you want a meal). Telephone: 01865 343240.
THE SEVEN STARS, Marsh Baldon. Picturesque setting on edge of The Green. Telephone: 01865 343255.
MOUNTS BAY INN, Nuneham Courtenay. Telephone: 01865 340202.
 There is also a post office and foodstore in Nuneham Courtenay.

Walk 3
ABINGDON
Length 5½ miles

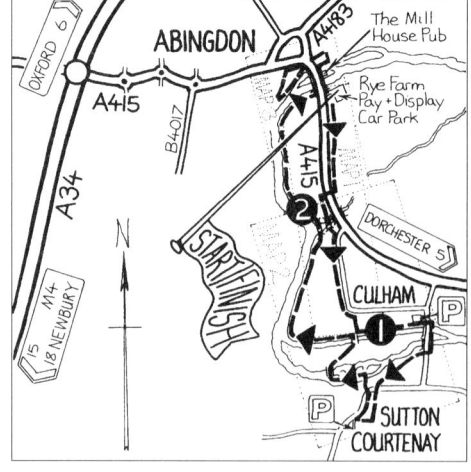

GETTING THERE: Take the A34 from Reading or Oxford, turn off at Abingdon and follow the signs to the town centre. From here follow the A415 towards Dorchester, go over the bridge and then take your first left into Rye Farm pay and display car park. You may find some free parking on Sundays on the town side of the bridge.

MOORING: Downstream of Abindgon Bridge.

TERRAIN: Flat and generally good surfaces except lengths beside the Thames in wet weather.

START: (GR 500967) From the car park return to the A415, turn left away from Abingdon and walk along the raised pavement on the left hand side.

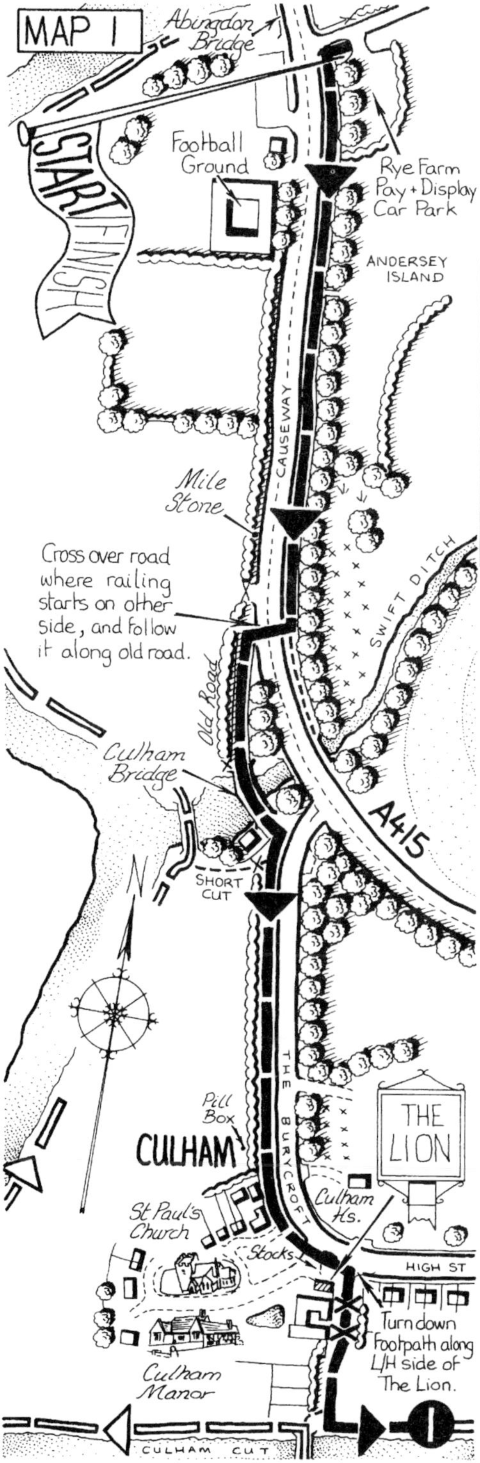

MAP 1

Abingdon Bridge

START/FINISH

Football Ground

Rye Farm Pay + Display Car Park

ANDERSEY ISLAND

CAUSEWAY

Mile Stone

Cross over road where railing starts on other side, and follow it along old road.

Old Road

SWIFT DITCH

Culham Bridge

A415

SHORT CUT

THE BURY CROFT

Pill Box

CULHAM

St Paul's Church

Stocks

Culham Hs.

HIGH ST

THE LION

Turn down footpath along L/H side of The Lion.

Culham Manor

CULHAM CUT

1

SHORT CUTS: This walk can easily be divided into two shorter walks (bottom half 3 miles, top half 2½ miles) by using the footpath just below Culham Bridge. If you walk the bottom half only, then park at either of the free car parks marked on the area map and use Map 2.

Culham Bridge

INTRODUCTION: Ancient buildings abound on this Thames-side trip through two picturesque villages and the forgotten County Town of Berkshire! There are elongated almshouses, a church which is wider than it is long, an 800 year old chimney, and one of the oldest domestic houses in the country. Also discover a lost road, a battle site, the dramatic Sutton Pools, and finish at a pub hanging on to the middle of Abingdon Bridge!

THE CAUSEWAY: The road and raised path from Abingdon to Culham Bridge is a causeway constructed from 1416-1422 by the Guild of the Holy Cross. Along with the bridges, the new route drew valuable traffic which previously passed through Wallingford to the commercial benefit of Abingdon.

In the 18th century it became a turnpike road (notice the old milestone) and then in 1928 the new Culham Bridge was constructed, leaving a short stretch of the original route lost in the trees (which you walk along up to the old bridge).

MAP 2

CULHAM BRIDGE: Built at the same time as the Causeway to replace the old ford, this medieval bridge is now a scheduled ancient monument. This comes after two pill boxes and a concrete platform were built on it in the Second World War! (You can tell that the parapet on the north side is a modern repair made when these were removed.) Although it saw no action in the 1940s it had previously been the scene of a battle three hundred years earlier.

It was January 1645 and the Parliamentarians were just hanging on to their base of Abingdon, surrounded as they were by the Royalists at Wallingford, Faringdon and the King himself at Oxford. His son Prince Rupert led a force to recapture Abingdon across Culham Bridge and along

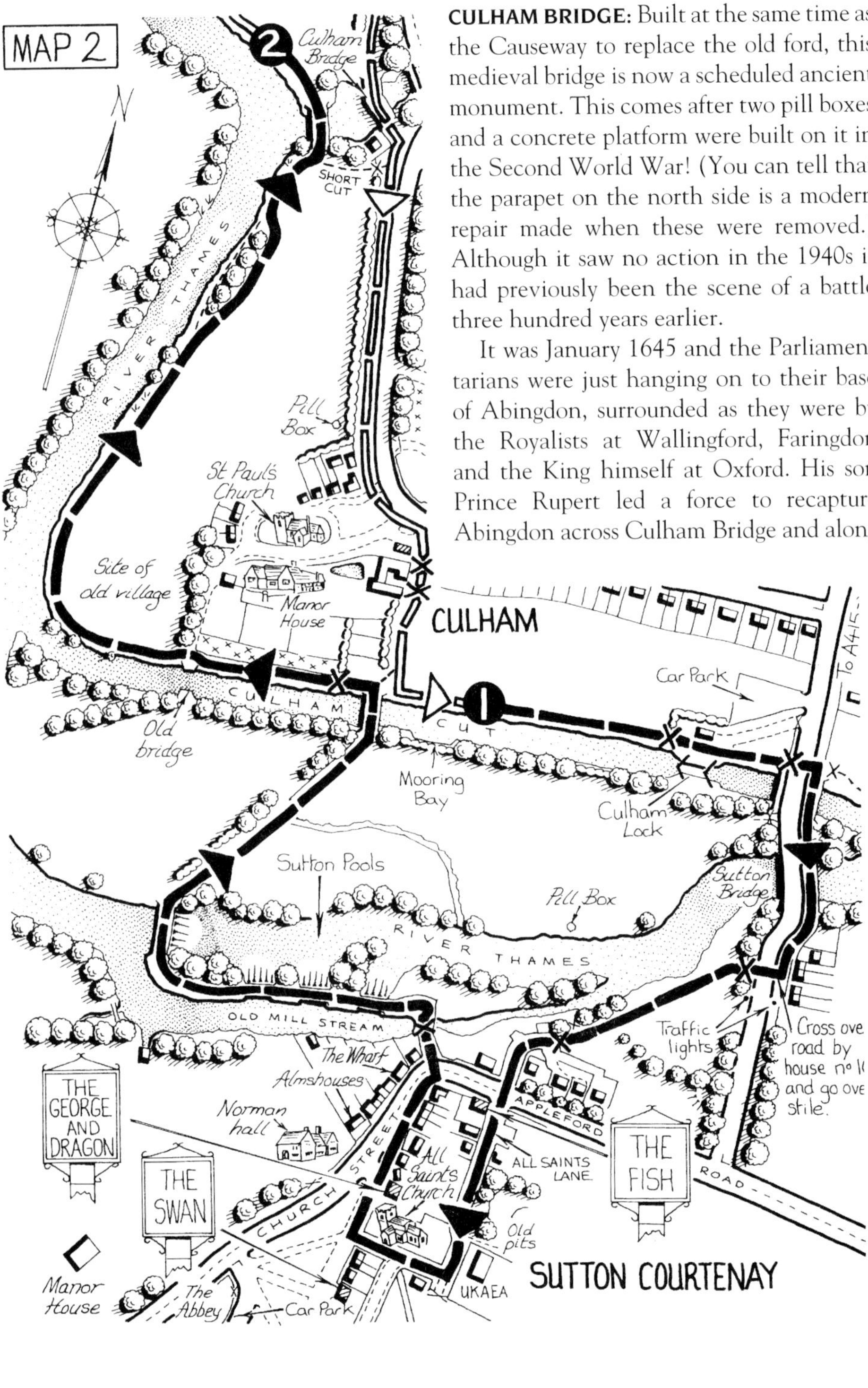

All Saints Church,
Sutton Courtenay.

Norman
Window (on
south side
of tower).

the Causeway. Unfortunately the winter flooding meant that Rupert's troops had to progress in a narrow line along the road while the defenders hidden in the surrounding water could pick them off at will. The Royalists were forced to retreat and although they tried another attack the following year, they never regained Abingdon.

CULHAM: The original village centred around the manor and church, with old roads and buildings discovered on aerial photographs to the west by the Thames. Culham Cut was constructed in 1809 and along with the enclosures and the building of High Street it shifted the village to the east.

Culham Manor was a grange, that is a farm run by a monastic order, in this case Abingdon Abbey. Culham House is Georgian but hidden mainly behind its later gar-

den wall, while the most notable feature of the church is an excessively tall chimney!

SUTTON COURTENAY: An idyllic setting of church, pubs and cottages surrounding a triangular green makes the effort to reach it well worthwhile. Unusually, the three largest private houses are all of genuine antiquity.

Thatch or Tile?
Sutton Courtenay

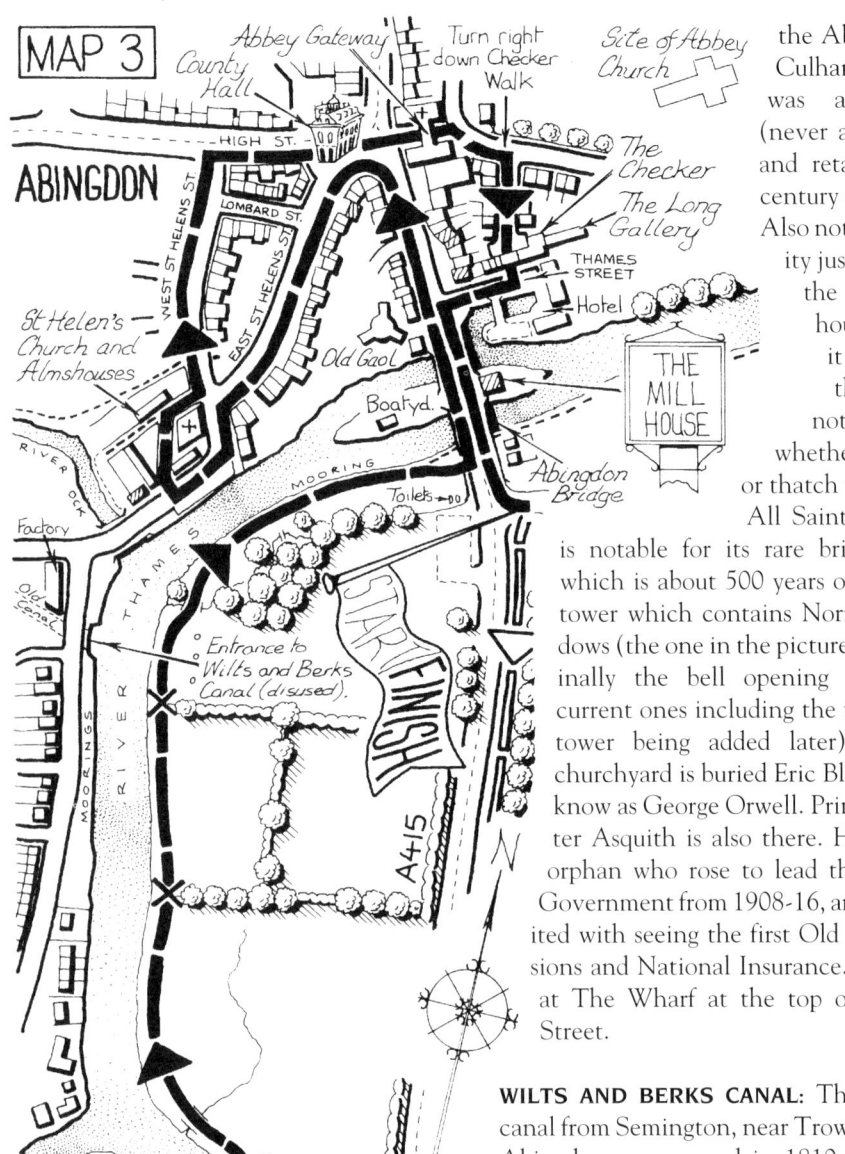

MAP 3

ABINGDON

Abbey Gateway • County Hall

Turn right down Checker Walk

Site of Abbey Church

HIGH ST.

LOMBARD ST.

WEST ST HELENS ST.

EAST ST HELENS ST.

St Helen's Church and Almshouses

The Checker

The Long Gallery

THAMES STREET

Hotel

THE MILL HOUSE

Old Gaol

Boatyd.

Abingdon Bridge

MOORING

Toilets →

RIVER OCK

Factory

Old canal

THAMES

Entrance to Wilts and Berks Canal (disused).

MOORINGS

RIVER

STARFINISH

A415

N

The Norman Hall dates from the 1190s, making it one of the oldest domestic buildings in the country. The Manor House to the south was the home of the Courtenays and dates in part back to the 1200s, while the Abbey, like Culham Manor, was a grange (never an abbey) and retains 14th century elements. Also note an oddity just north of the Swan: a house where it appears they could not decide whether to tile or thatch the roof!

All Saints' church is notable for its rare brick porch which is about 500 years old and its tower which contains Norman windows (the one in the picture was originally the bell opening with the current ones including the top of the tower being added later). In the churchyard is buried Eric Blair, better know as George Orwell. Prime Minister Asquith is also there. He was an orphan who rose to lead the Liberal Government from 1908-16, and is credited with seeing the first Old Age Pensions and National Insurance. He lived at The Wharf at the top of Church Street.

WILTS AND BERKS CANAL: This narrow canal from Semington, near Trowbridge, to Abingdon was opened in 1810 with coal and farm produce being the main goods transported. Within thirty years it was in commercial decline due to the railways and it was finally abandoned in 1914. You can see where it joined the Thames just downstream of the metal bridge over the River Ock (built for the canal company). There is corrugated iron sheeting blocking the old

County Hall, Abingdon.

which were large enough to be termed a town) was discovered in the 1980s, Abingdon has been described as the oldest town in the country! The first major building here was the Abbey which was founded in AD 675 and at its height in around 1100 was one of the largest in the country. Despite its importance to Abingdon, the relationship between the monks and the townsfolk was strained and riots in 1327 led to the sacking of the Abbey and in return the hanging of the twelve ringleaders. The only true remains of the Abbey are the Long Gallery and the Checker (the old Abbey exchequer) which has a rare 13th century chimney. There is also the Abbey Gateway opposite the County Hall, the right hand arch of which was only created in the 19th century by knocking out the old lock-up to make it look symmetrical!

The diversion of the London to Gloucester road through the town after the building of the bridge and Causeway in 1422 brought valuable passing trade which helped it through the barren times after the later dissolution of the Abbey.

Abingdon's commercial importance can be measured by the magnificent County

entrance and behind it the brick factory was built at an angle in line with the course of the canal.

ABINGDON BRIDGE: Built in 1416 and only partly widened in 1928 so it still narrows halfway across!

OLD GOAL: This old prison was opened in 1811 and the suffering continues today as it is now a local leisure centre!

ABINGDON: This once County Town of Berkshire has now been relegated to the southern end of Oxfordshire but retains the dignified buildings of its former status.

Since what is believed to have been an Iron Age oppidum (earliest settlements

---

REFRESHMENTS:

THE MILL HOUSE This dramatically positioned pub, halfway along Abingdon Bridge, was previously called the Nag's Head. In its current guise it offers food and drink for all the family, all day, with balcony and garden seating overlooking the Thames. Telephone: 01235 536645.

There are numerous other pubs and restaurants around the town centre.

If you walk the bottom half then there are three pubs in Sutton Courtenay, the George and Dragon being noted for its atmosphere and Sunday lunch! Telephone: 01235 848142.

Hall, an acclaimed masterpiece built by Wren's master mason, Christopher Kempster, from 1678-82. South from it runs East St Helens Street which is lined with a colourful display of notable houses including the King's Head and Bell pub, the Georgian Twickenham House and No 26 which dates from the 15th century. This leads to St Helen's church which is notable for being wider than it is long. Behind it are three almshouses, the most important being Long Alley of 1446 with its seemingly endless timber cloister. To the north is the pretty single-storeyed Twitty's Almshouse which was built in 1707, and alongside the river is the Brick Alley Almshouse of 1718.

The survival of all these is due in no small part to the obstruction to Brunel's plans to make the town a major railway centre by local landlords. Its late and minor entry on the transport map was to Reading's benefit which took over the mantle of County Town in 1869. (There are guide books which give a more detailed history available from the Tourist Information Office in front of the Old Goal.)

Long Alley Almshouses, Abingdon.

DORCHESTER

Length 4 miles

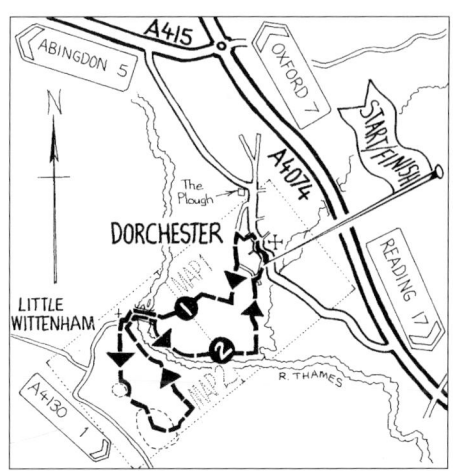

Abbey and Tollhouse, Dorchester.

GETTING THERE: Dorchester is just off the A4074 Oxford to Reading road about 4 miles north of Wallingford. If approaching from Oxford turn right onto the A415 towards Abingdon, then turn immediately left, signposted to Dorchester. After a mile turn right at the T junction and continue through the town until just past the Abbey and before the bridge approach turn right down Bridge End. You will find parking and toilets immediately on the left. From Reading turn left just after Shillingford and after passing over the bridge turn left into Bridge End.

MOORING: Below Day's Lock.

TERRAIN: One steep climb up Round Hill, otherwise flat. Damp rather than muddy.

START: (GR 578941) From the parking area walk towards the Abbey and then turn left and follow the High Street.

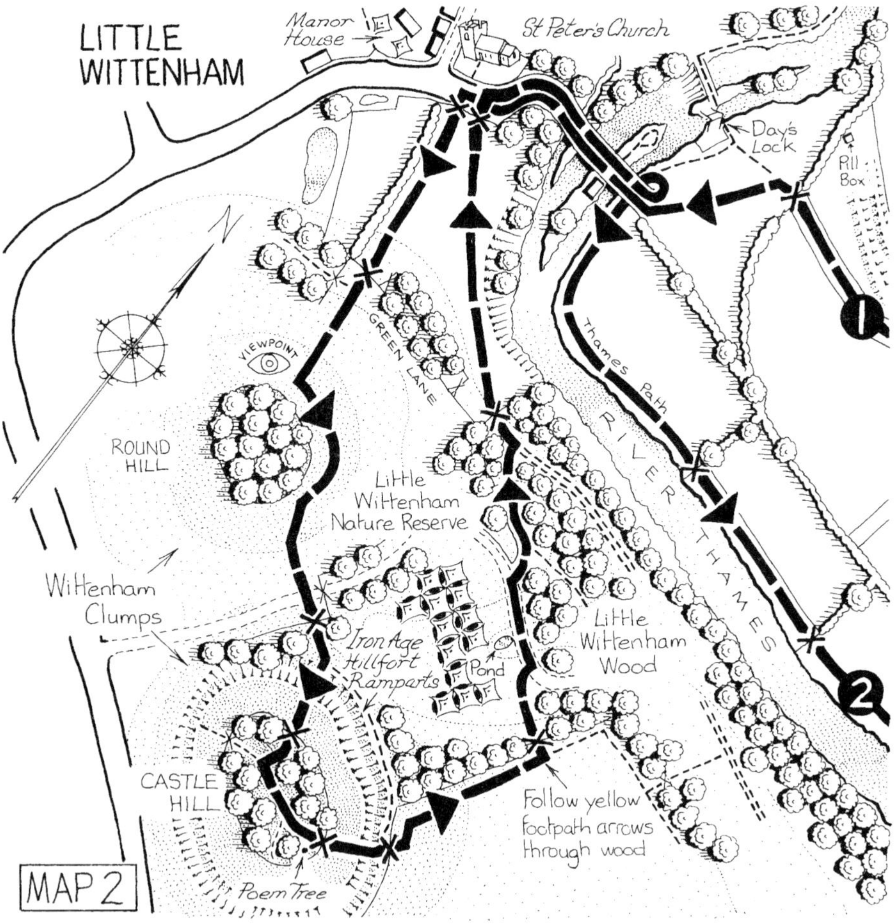

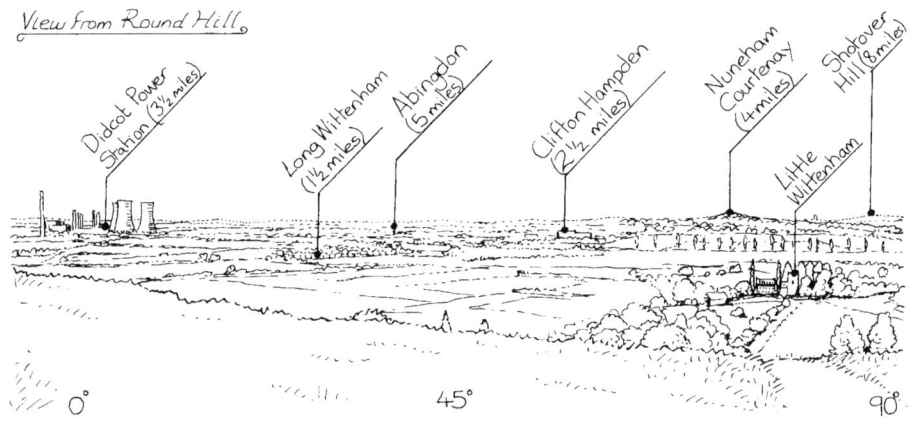

LITTLE WITTENHAM

Manor House

St Peter's Church

Day's Lock

Pill Box

1

N

VIEWPOINT

GREEN LANE

ROUND HILL

Little Wittenham Nature Reserve

Thames Path

RIVER THAMES

Wittenham Clumps

Iron Age Hillfort Ramparts

Pond

Little Wittenham Wood

2

CASTLE HILL

Follow yellow footpath arrows through wood

Poem Tree

MAP 2

View from Round Hill

Didcot Power Station (3½ miles)

Long Wittenham (1½ miles)

Abingdon (5 miles)

Clifton Hampden (2½ miles)

Nuneham Courtenay (4 miles)

Shotover Hill (8 miles)

Little Wittenham

0°   45°   90°

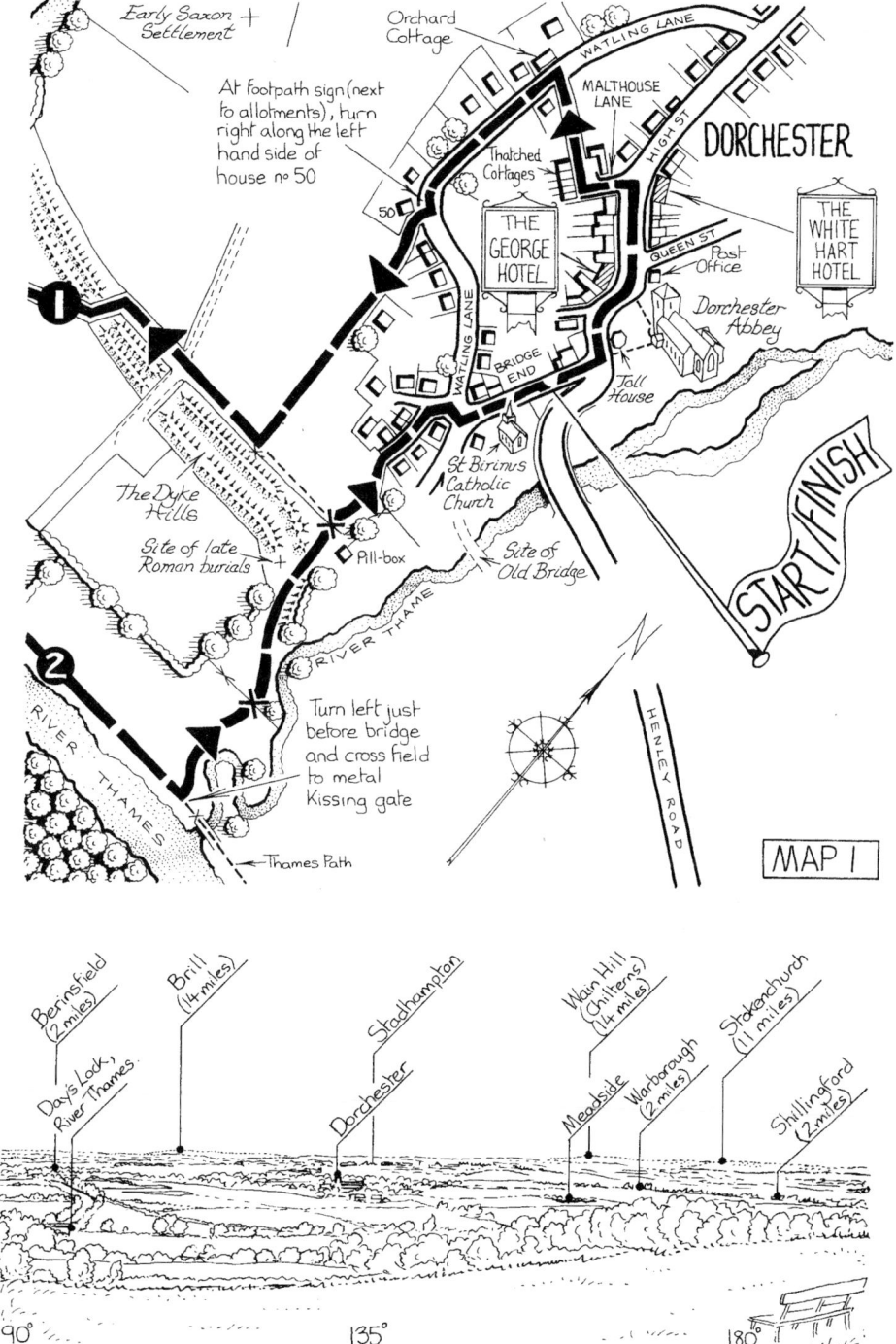

Early Saxon Settlement +

At footpath sign (next to allotments), turn right along the left hand side of house no 50

Orchard Cottage

WATLING LANE

MALTHOUSE LANE

HIGH ST

DORCHESTER

Thatched Cottages

50

THE GEORGE HOTEL

WATLING LANE

QUEEN ST

Post Office

THE WHITE HART HOTEL

Dorchester Abbey

BRIDGE END

Toll House

The Dyke Hills

Site of late Roman burials

Pill-box

St Birinus Catholic Church

RIVER THAME

Site of Old Bridge

START/FINISH

HENLEY ROAD

2

RIVER THAMES

Turn left just before bridge and cross field to metal Kissing gate

Thames Path

MAP 1

Berinsfield (2 miles)

Brill (14 miles)

Stadhampton

Wain Hill (Chilterns) (14 miles)

Stokenchurch (11 miles)

Day's Lock, River Thames

Dorchester

Meadside

Warborough (2 miles)

Shillingford (2 miles)

90°   135°   180°

INTRODUCTION: Few walks in Southern England pass through such a historically rich landscape. There have been Neolithic monuments, an Iron Age hillfort, a Roman town and a cathedral church overseeing one of the largest bishoprics in the country. Dorchester may no longer be as important, but the remains of its former glory can still be found along this walk. In addition to all this antiquity you will see dramatic views, a nature reserve, the attractive setting around Day's Lock and a wealth of timber-framed cottages and old coaching inns.

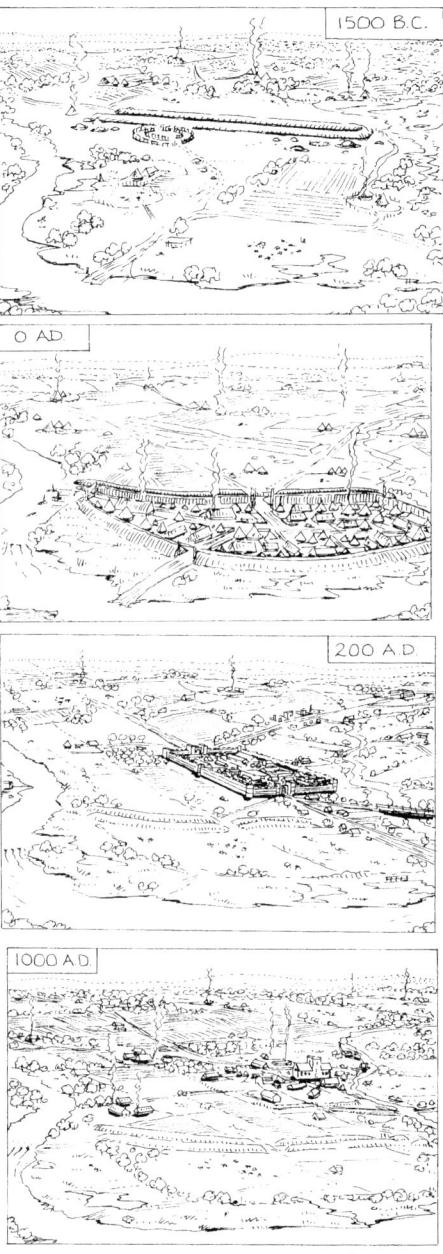

DORCHESTER: These four views over Dorchester help show the development of the town through the ages (although the features shown would not have been in use at the same time). The first one shows the mysterious long banks called a Curcus which was constructed between 3000-2000 BC for a purpose we cannot yet understand. The big circles in front of it are a henge monument which was erected in the millennium after.

In the view of the first century AD you can see the Iron Age 'oppidum' which was a substantial settlement of 46 hectares. This replaced the earlier and much smaller hillfort on Castle Hill. The interior has revealed numerous pits, huts and roads and contained one of the largest concentrations of Iron Age coins in the country. It probably lasted less than 100 years as the invading Romans built first a fort and then a new walled town to the north. The remains of the 'oppidum' are now known as Dyke Hills.

By AD 200 this small Roman town had walls with towers and many of the earlier timber houses had been replaced by stone buildings. The west line of the town can today be traced along Watling Lane and the bend in the road by No 50 follows the corner of the walls nearest to you in the picture.

By AD 1000 the church set up by St Biri-nus was the seat of a vast 'see' stretching up as far as the Humber. The settlement around would have supported this ecclesiastical establishment and the nearby Bishops Court. Later, by the 17th century, the town took its present shape from the importance of the London to Gloucester road which led to the building of the numerous coaching inns.

DORCHESTER ABBEY: In AD 635 on the banks of the River Thame, Oswald, the Christian King of the then mighty Northumbria, and Cynegils, King of the West Saxons (Wessex), met to celebrate the marriage of the former to the latter's daughter. Part of the arrangement was that the pagan king of Wessex would become a Christian, and this baptism was conducted by Birinus, a missionary sent by the Pope to convert the English to the faith. As a reward for his services Birinus was given Dorchester for his episcopal see and hereabouts built and dedicated his cathedral church. Unfortunately, Cynegils's son Cenwalh had a communication problem with the next Bishop, Agilbert, (they did not speak the same language). So the King moved the bishopric to Winchester in the 660s without consulting the Frenchman! This change may also have been forced on Cenwalh by the advancing Mercians led by Penda. The Mercian leader was offended by Cenwalh who had cheated on his wife; she just happening to be Penda's daughter!

Dorchester regained importance when in AD 869 the Bishop moved here after the Danish invasion. Yet again, in the 1070s, the seat was moved, this time to Lincoln, and the role Dorchester had played as an important centre for thousands of years started to wane. Nevertheless, in 1140 the old church was refounded as an Augustinian Abbey and the present building began to take shape. The most notable work was after 1293 when huge amounts of money were lavished on the Abbey, including the three windows at the east end, of which the famous Jesse Window is of European architectural importance.

There is a detailed history of the building available within the Abbey. While you are there try and find the grave of Sarah Fletcher whose reason for death in a more sexist age was given as 'Excessive Sensibility'!

Away from the Abbey, down Bridge End, is the little Catholic Church of St Birinus. It was built in 1849 by W. W. Wardell who later emigrated in Australia and built the great Catholic cathedrals in Sydney and Melbourne. Bridge End used to be the main road leading down to the site of the old bridge but this was replaced by the present one in 1816, around which time the tollhouse was also built.

LITTLE WITTENHAM: A tiny village straggling along the road to Day's Lock which is dominated by the Manor House with its two huge redwood trees and the pretty, if over restored, church.

The nature reserve which encompasses the Clumps has a guide which you can pick up at the entrance for a donation. This will point out the Iron Age hillfort which was made redundant when the Dyke Hills were constructed and the Poem Tree which was carved by Joseph Tubb in 1844.

REFRESHMENTS:

THE GEORGE HOTEL. Started life as a brewhouse for the Abbey and now offers excellent food and drinks all day. Telephone: 01865 340404.

THE FLEUR DE LYS. Opposite the Abbey and also of great character, offering fresh home-cooked food. Telephone: 01865 340502.

THE WHITE HART HOTEL. Telephone: 01865 340074.

Walk 5
BLEWBURY
Length 4 miles

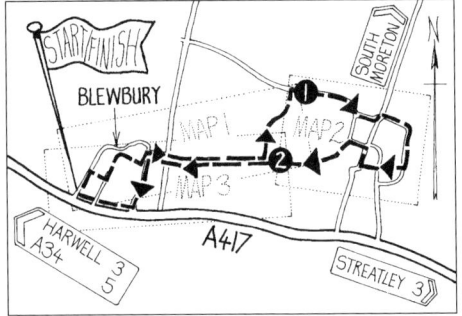

GETTING THERE: If heading south from Oxford on the A34 turn off onto the A4130 and go right towards Wantage, while if heading north use the A4185. Both roads meet at a roundabout where you take the A417 towards Reading. After about 4 miles you reach Blewbury where just past Sebastapol Wines you turn left up Westbrook Street. Park along the first hundred yards on the left hand side of the road.

TERRAIN: All on the level except for the optional short climb up Blewburton Hill.

START: (GR 527856) Walk up Westbrook Street away from the A417 and turn right down the footpath beside Forge Cottage.

INTRODUCTION: In an area renowned for nuclear research, railways, motor sports and the production of electricity it comes as a surprise to find ancient and untouched villages. This walk meanders through the maze of narrow lanes and paths which form Blewbury, then heads past the prominent hill with its spectacular views of the Thames Valley. After wandering through the

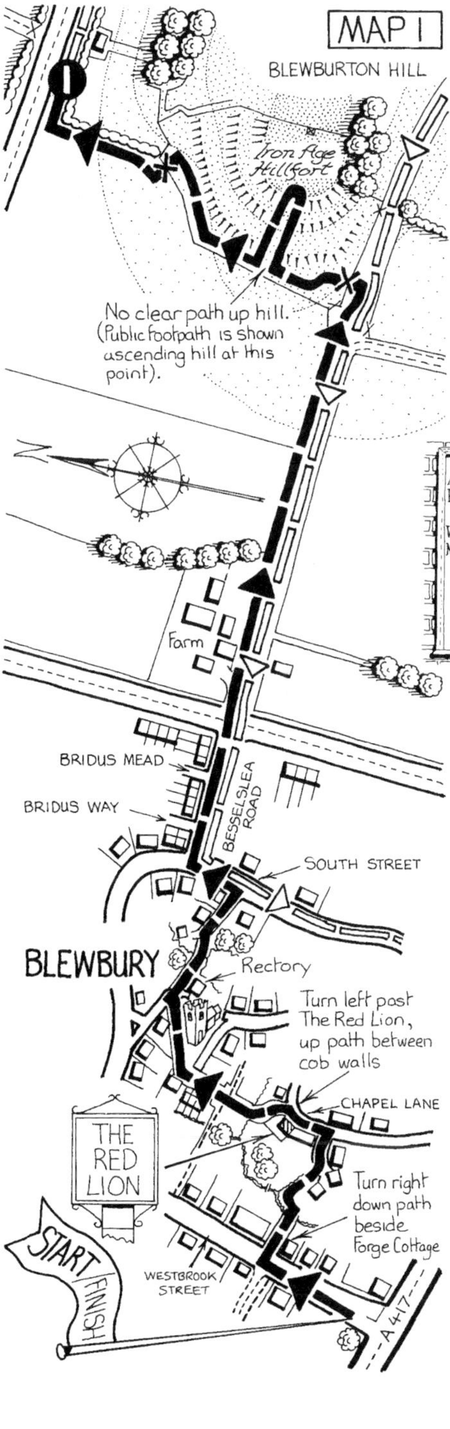

Astons you return to the rewarding choice of four pubs!

BLEWBURY: Although this richly historic village shows evidence of occupation over the past thousand years the immediate area can take you back even further. On the hills above are Bronze Age barrows, Iron Age ditches and even a Roman temple! In Blewbury itself is a Norman church, a medieval moated site and seemingly endless timber-framed cottages, mainly from the 16th and 17th centuries. It is the picturesque setting that these create which attracted Kenneth Grahame, author of *Wind in the Willows*, here (although A.A. Milne declined to rent his house, allegedly due to mice!).

On your walk through the village look out for the cob and thatch walls which mark out farmyards. One has a door dated 1823 from which the farmer used to sneak out for a quick pint at the Red Lion! Also on your left just before the church is a miniature detached cottage which was built as an almshouse for the oldest man in the village, while to the right is the impressive William Malthus Chantry School of 1709.

BLEWBURTON HILLFORT: It was built from

MAP I

BLEWBURTON HILL

Iron Age Hillfort

No clear path up hill. (Public footpath is shown ascending hill at this point).

N

Farm

BRIDUS MEAD

BRIDUS WAY

BESSELSLEA ROAD

SOUTH STREET

BLEWBURY

Rectory

Turn left past The Red Lion, up path between cob walls

CHAPEL LANE

THE RED LION

Turn right down path beside Forge Cottage

START FINISH

WESTBROOK STREET

A 417

A Charity School Built and Endowed by the Gift of WILLIAM MALTHUS Merchant Anᵒ Domini 1709.

Cob walls in Blewbury.

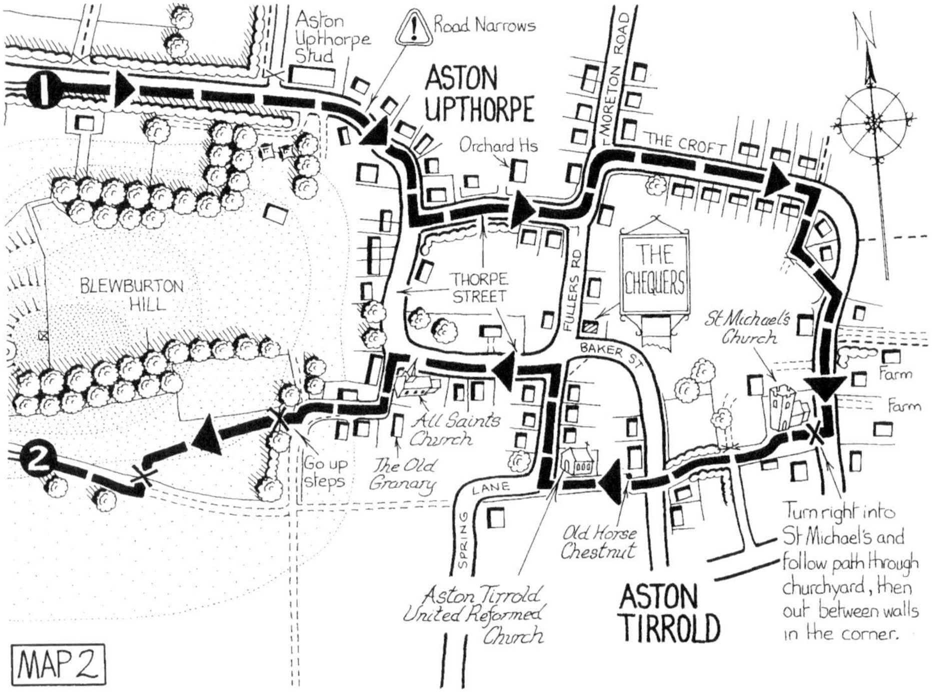

Aston Upthorpe Stud

⚠ Road Narrows

ASTON UPTHORPE

MORETON ROAD

THE CROFT

Orchard Hs

THE CHEQUERS

FULLERS RD

St Michael's Church

BAKER ST.

THORPE STREET

BLEWBURTON HILL

Farm

Farm

All Saints Church

Go up steps

The Old Granary

SPRING LANE

Old Horse Chestnut

Aston Tirrold United Reformed Church

ASTON TIRROLD

Turn right into St Michael's and follow path through churchyard, then out between walls in the corner.

MAP 2

400-300 BC with an external ditch and internal bank faced with timber. There was a large gateway and inside there would have been circular huts. Its demise in the early 1st century AD must have been sudden and violent as archaeologists found animals crushed beneath the collapsed walls and the burnt remains of the gateway!

ASTON UPTHORPE AND TIRROLD: This is where legend has it that King Ethelred heard mass while his younger brother Alfred (later Alfred the Great) was under pressure in the vital Battle of Ashdown. He said he would not move to aid his brother until mass had finished as he would not serve man before God. The actual site of the brothers' victory is probably nearer Uffington but they may have visited here earlier.

Today the villages seem as one with the north to south road splitting them in two. As in Blewbury the roads seem to wander between old timber-framed and brick houses with no clear centre of the community. There are three churches, of which the humble United Reformed church of 1728 is

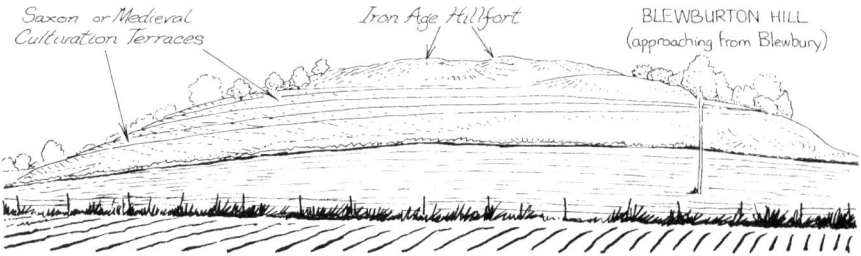

Saxon or Medieval Cultivation Terraces   Iron Age Hillfort   BLEWBURTON HILL (approaching from Blewbury)

of note due to its early date and simple symmetrical front. Also of note is the old granary behind All Saints' church which is still on the stone posts that prevented vermin getting access to the stored grain.

The biggest influence on the village today is horse racing. The Aston Upthorpe Stud has been developed over many years by the brothers Sheikh Mohammed and then Sheikh Ahmed al Maktoum into one of the leading stud farms in England.

THE BLEWBURY MISER: In 1781 the parish of Blewbury was given to the Rev John Keble (whose son went on to initiate the Oxford Movement and had Keble College, Oxford named after him). John already had a parish so appointed the Rev Morgan Jones to the post where he was to stay for 43 years but gain a reputation as a miser. He had only one meal and cup of tea each week and wore only one coat for all of those years. When he overheard someone comment on his 'addiction to free ale' he was so offended he gave it up for life! Such was his notoriety that Dickens based his character of Blackberry Jones from *Our Mutual Friend* on him. (Morgan actually removed blackberry briars from graves to save buying firewood!) When he died he left the then huge sum of £18,000 to relatives while the villagers kept some of his possessions as they had grown fond of him despite his frugal nature.

REFRESHMENTS:

THE RED LION. Atmospheric pub in an attractive setting at the end of Nottingham Fee. Telephone: 01235 850403.

THE BLEWBURY INN. With à la carte restaurant. Telephone: 01235 850496..

THE LOAD OF MISCHIEF. Telephone: 01235 850281.

THE BARLEY MOW. Telephone: 01235 850296.

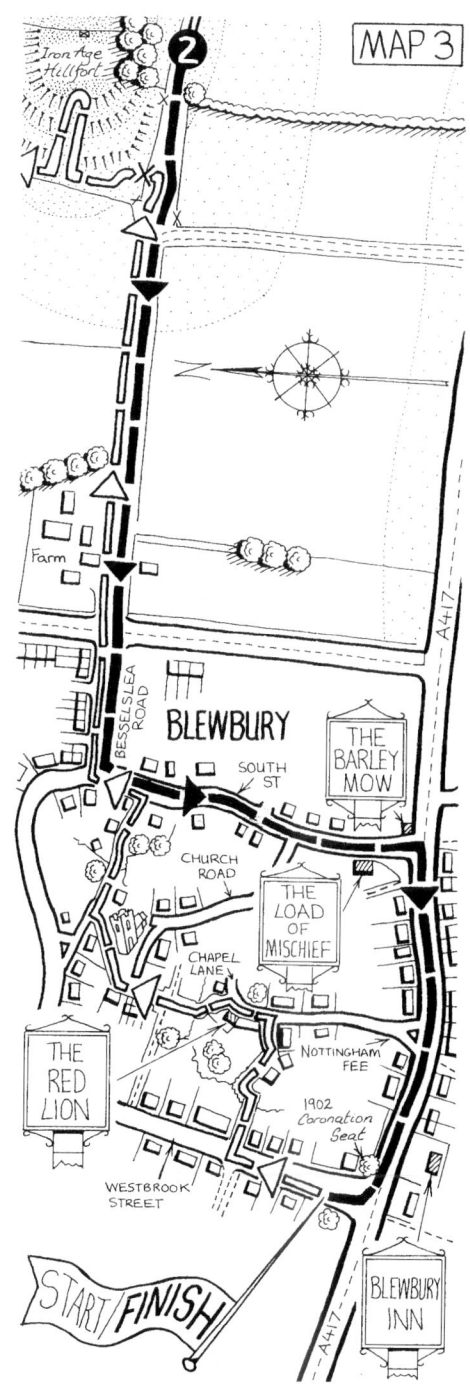

Walk 6
WALLINGFORD
Length 4¼ miles

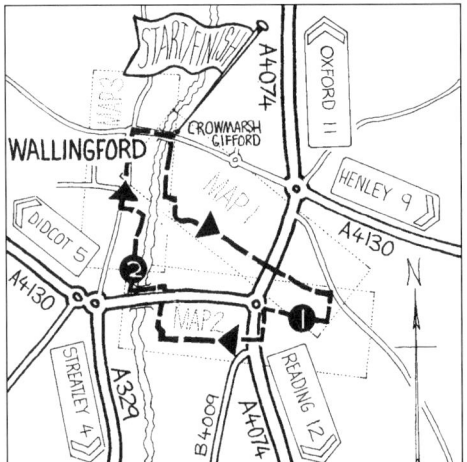

GETTING THERE: From Oxford head down the A4074, past Benson and then turn right at the Crowmarsh Roundabout towards Wallingford. (If coming up from Reading then turn left at this roundabout.) Drive through Crowmarsh Gifford and then just before the traffic lights on Wallingford Bridge turn right into the pay and display car park.

MOORING: Below Wallingford Bridge.

TERRAIN: One steady climb; boots essential along the Ridgeway (for ankle protection!).

START: (GR 611894) From the car park head across the grass to the river, then turn left and follow the bank under the bridge.

INTRODUCTION: 'How are the mighty fallen'! Wallingford was founded as a fortified town by King Alfred and visited by

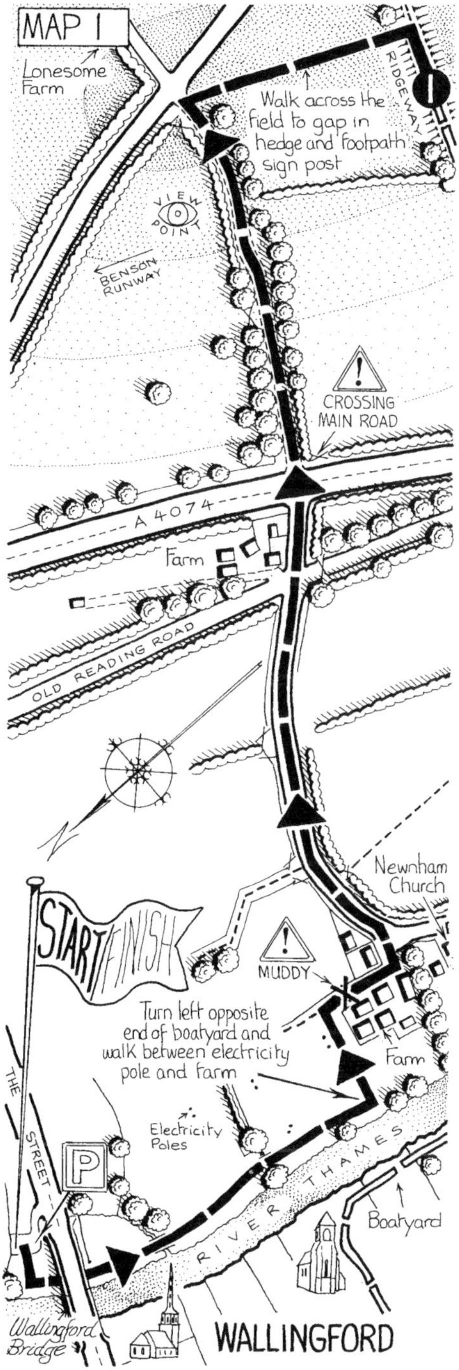
MAP 1
Lonesome Farm
Walk across the field to gap in hedge and footpath sign post
RIDGEWAY
VIEW POINT
BENSON RUNWAY
CROSSING MAIN ROAD
A 4074
Farm
OLD READING ROAD
N
START/FINISH
Newnham Church
MUDDY
Turn left opposite end of boatyard and walk between electricity pole and farm
Farm
Electricity Poles
THE STREET
P
RIVER THAMES
Boatyard
Wallingford Bridge
WALLINGFORD

Wallingford Bridge

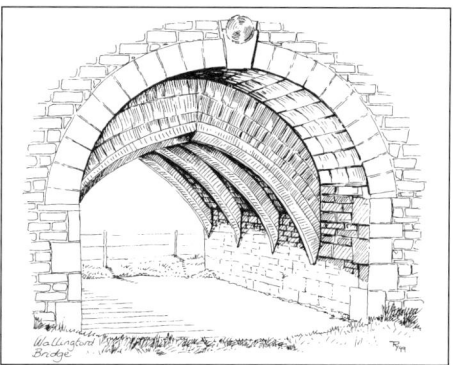

William the Conqueror, the feuding King Stephen and Empress Matilda. The castle was one of the last Royalist strongholds to surrender in 1646. But decline since the 14th century has today left it one of the quieter Thames-side towns. This walk not only visits its historic centre but also a ruined church, Grim's Ditch and a commanding viewpoint.

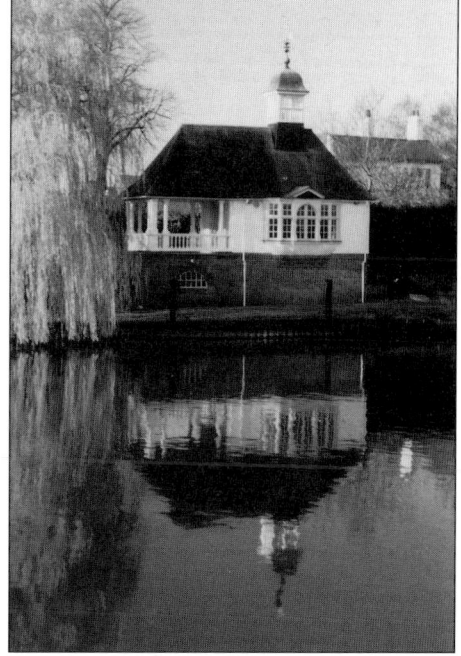

An attractive summer-house by the Thames.

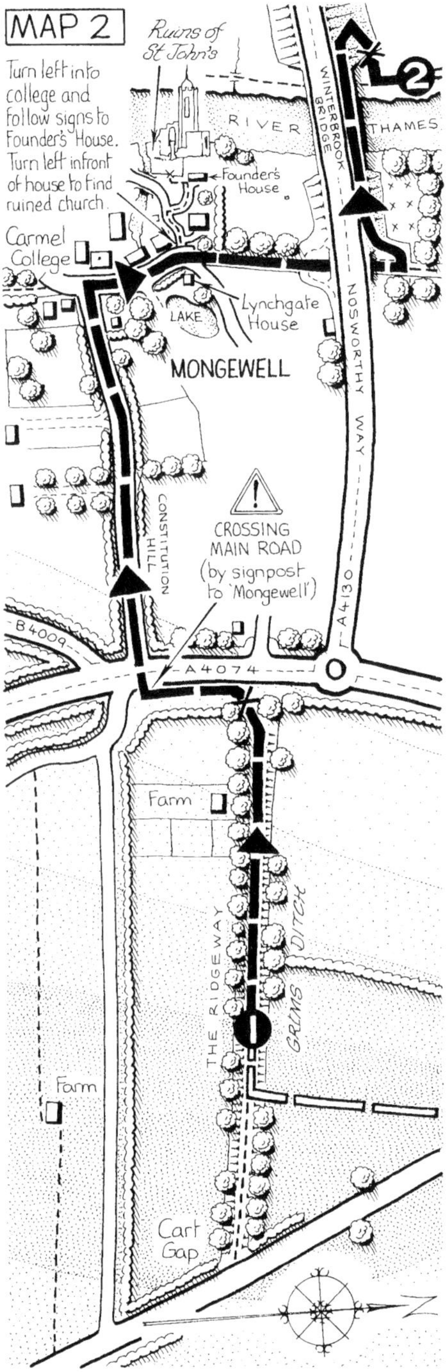

MAP 2

Ruins of St John's

Turn left into college and follow signs to Founders' House. Turn left in front of house to find ruined church

Carmel College

RIVER THAMES

WINTERBROOK BRIDGE

Founder's House

Lynchgate House

LAKE

MONGEWELL

NOSWORTHY WAY

A4130

CONSTITUTION HILL

⚠ CROSSING MAIN ROAD (by signpost to 'Mongewell')

B4009

A4074

Farm

THE RIDGEWAY

GRIMS DITCH

Farm

Cart Gap

WALLINGFORD BRIDGE: Its 19 arches make it almost as long as the original London Bridge and it has lasted better! Its present form was the result of rebuilding in 1810 but under one of the arches you can see the ribs of the narrower original medieval bridge. Some moulded stones can be seen which came from the old Priory Church which was demolished and used for repairs after its dissolution in 1528.

CHALMORE LOCK: Just past where the footpath leaves the Thames is the site of a lock and weir, used to save water in summer and only lasting fifty years with it being removed in 1883.

NEWNHAM CHURCH: A picturesque Norman church next to the equally attractive Old Farm House. Within is a brass to Letitia Barnard which has been pierced by a bullet, shot during the siege of Wallingford in 1646.

Ruins of St John's Church, Mongewell.

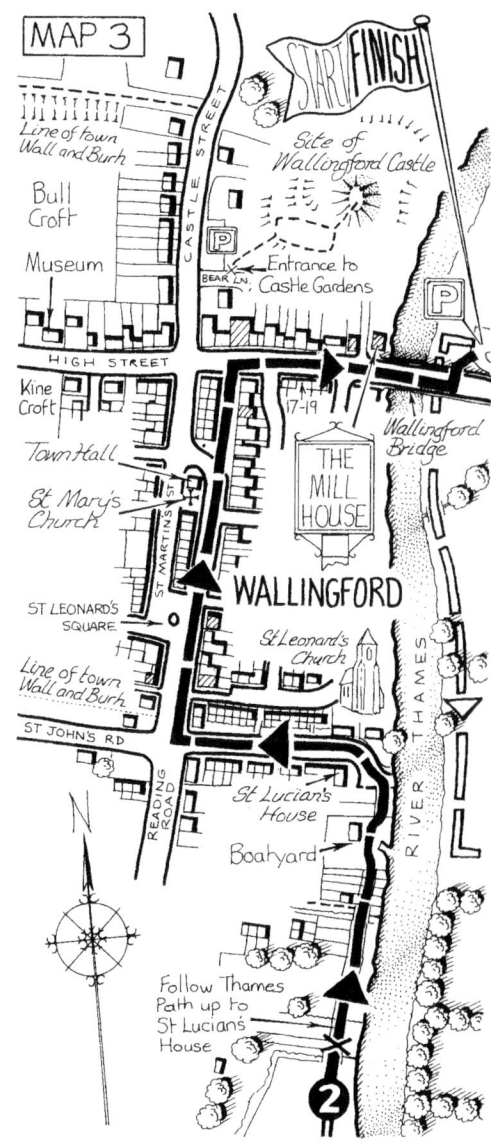

REFRESHMENTS:
THE MILL HOUSE. A popular pub for the whole family, with good food and an idyllic setting overlooking the Thames. Telephone: 01491 834100.

There are numerous other pubs in the town centre.

GRIM'S DITCH: This bank and ditch (you actually walk along the top of the bank) have long been believed to be Saxon. Recent archaeology though has dated similar features in Oxfordshire to the Late Iron Age. It was possibly a boundary feature to mark the territory of the Catuvellauni, the most powerful tribe in pre-Roman Southern Britain.

MONGEWELL: An old estate which became Carmel College in 1953. The original Georgian building stood in the area above Founder's House (retaining walls and a monument in the field by the bypass relate to this earlier house). It was replaced in 1889 and this later house is incorporated within the college and its slightly bizarre gathering of buildings. Most eye catching is the pyramidal boathouse which can be seen from the footpath leading to the ruined church, St John's.

The church was rebuilt in Gothic style for Bishop Shute Barrington who owned the estate in 1791. He added the brick turret and apse which were probably designed by James Wyatt who was working for the Bishop in Salisbury. Although the chancel and apse are still intact the remainder became ruinous in the 20th century.

WALLINGFORD: The town rose to prominence when it became one of King Alfred's 'burhs', which were fortified planned settlements forming a defensive line to keep out Danish invaders from Wessex. Remains still surround Kine Croft and Bull Croft to the west. William the Conqueror stopped here to receive homage from Archbishop Stigand on his way from the Battle of Hastings to London, and in the following year gave orders to build a motte and bailey castle at Wallingford.

In the dispute for the throne between the Empress Matilda and King Stephen in 1142 the former took refuge in the castle while the latter built fortifications on the other side of the river. It was here also that King Stephen finally agreed to let Henry, Matilda's son, succeed to the throne to become the first Plantagenet king.

From the 14th century Wallingford declined at an alarming rate due to plague and the diversion of the main London to Gloucester road to a route through Abingdon. Even in the last century there were doss houses here, like the Fat Ox where you could 'sleep on a line'. This was where a rope was strung across a room and men would drape their arms over it and sleep standing up!

A full history and guide book is available from the tourist information office under the Town Hall. Buildings of note include the 16th century St Lucian's House, the Town Hall of 1670 and St Peter's church with its 'wedding cake' style spire of 1777. Also note houses 17-19 High Street which were rebuilt in the 16th century but under which a basement dating to the 1300s remains! The castle grounds can be accessed via Bear Lane from 10 am to 6 pm (closed at 3 pm in winter).

Town Hall

Walk 7
GORING
Length 3 miles

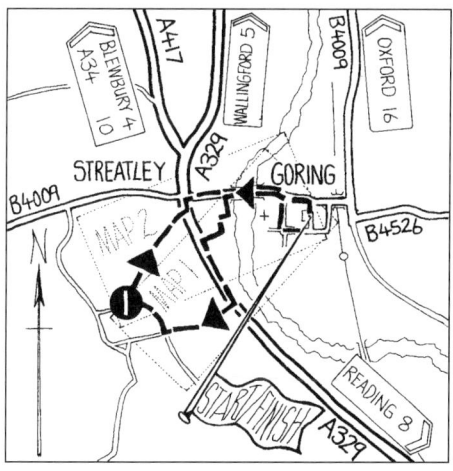

View over Goring

GETTING THERE: From the A329 between Reading and Wallingford turn off eastwards at Streatley onto the B4009. Drive over the bridge and then just before the shops go right down Manor Road, round a sharp left bend and then immediately after the Catherine Wheel pub turn left into the pay and display car park. There is free but limited parking at the start of Manor Road.

MOORING: Downstream of Goring Bridge.

TERRAIN: Flat, tarmacked roads through the villages but boots recommended for two moderate hill climbs and slippery slopes.

START: (GR 599807) From the car park walk up the path beside the toilet block and at the top turn left along the High Street.

SHORT CUT: 1½ miles. Turn right when you reach the A329 on Map 1 and rejoin the walk just before the Bull at Streatley on Map 2.

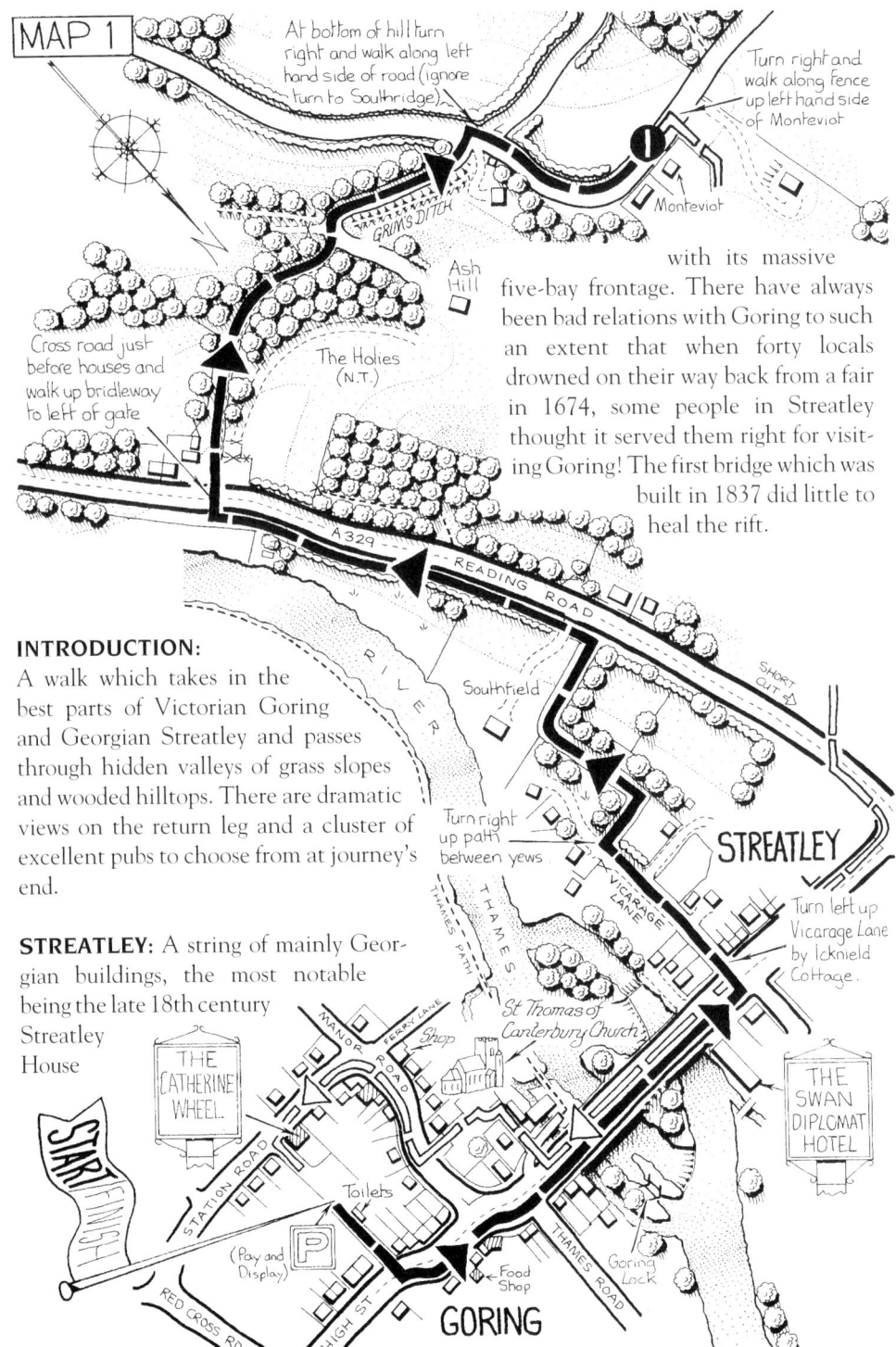

MAP 1

At bottom of hill turn right and walk along left hand side of road (ignore turn to Southridge).

Turn right and walk along fence up left hand side of Monteviot

Monteviot

GRIMS DITCH

Ash Hill

Cross road just before houses and walk up bridleway to left of gate

The Holies (N.T.)

A329

READING ROAD

SHORT CUT

INTRODUCTION:
A walk which takes in the best parts of Victorian Goring and Georgian Streatley and passes through hidden valleys of grass slopes and wooded hilltops. There are dramatic views on the return leg and a cluster of excellent pubs to choose from at journey's end.

with its massive five-bay frontage. There have always been bad relations with Goring to such an extent that when forty locals drowned on their way back from a fair in 1674, some people in Streatley thought it served them right for visiting Goring! The first bridge which was built in 1837 did little to heal the rift.

RIVER

Southfield

Turn right up path between yews

STREATLEY

VICARAGE LANE

Turn left up Vicarage Lane by Icknield Cottage.

STREATLEY: A string of mainly Georgian buildings, the most notable being the late 18th century Streatley House

THE CATHERINE WHEEL.

MANOR ROAD

FERRY LANE

Shop

St Thomas of Canterbury Church

THAMES PATH

THAMES

THE SWAN DIPLOMAT HOTEL

START/FINISH

STATION ROAD

Toilets

P (Pay and Display)

RED CROSS RD

HIGH ST

Food Shop

THAMES ROAD

Goring Lock

GORING

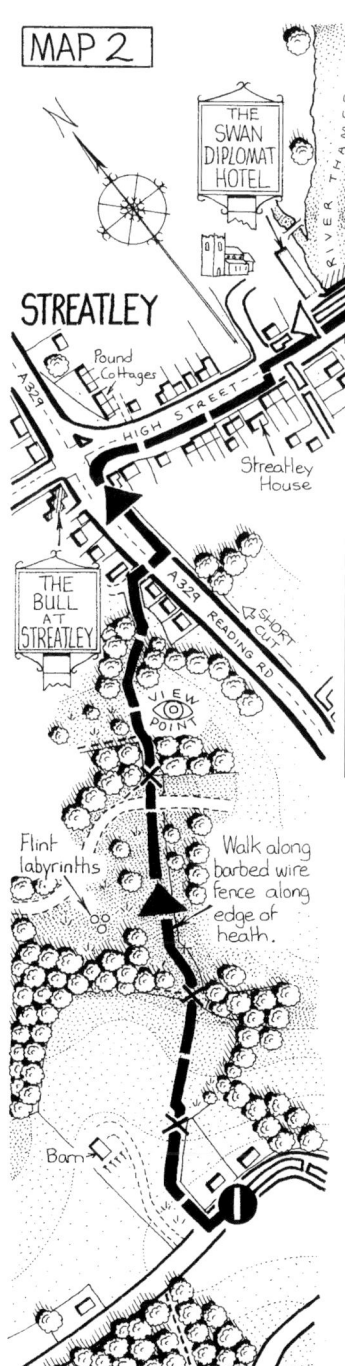

MAP 2

GORING

START FINISH

THE MILLER OF MANSFIELD

THE SWAN DIPLOMAT HOTEL

RIVER THAMES

HIGH ST

P

Toilets

THE CATHERINE WHEEL

MANOR ROAD

JOHN BARLEYCORN

STREATLEY

Pound Cottages

A329

HIGH STREET

Streatley House

Mill

Turn down steps, walk straight towards church, go left through gate and up through churchyard to Manor Road.

THE BULL AT STREATLEY

A329 READING RD

SHORT CUT

VIEW POINT

Flint labyrinths

Walk along barbed wire fence along edge of heath.

Barn

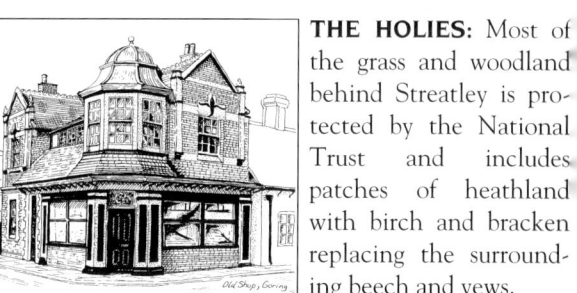

Old Shop, Goring

THE HOLIES: Most of the grass and woodland behind Streatley is protected by the National Trust and includes patches of heathland with birch and bracken replacing the surrounding beech and yews.

GORING: Now larger than its neighbour due to Victorian expansion with the coming of the railway. There are still some older buildings here, notably the church with its mainly Norman tower which was also the site of a priory. Along Station Road are some 16th and 17th century houses as this was once the main street in the village down to the ferry, before the bridge was built. Note the old Victorian shop on the corner of Ferry Lane with its glazed turrret.

REFRESHMENTS:

THE CATHERINE WHEEL. Pretty timber-framed building dating back to the 16th century. Noted for good food and service. Telephone: 01491 872379.

JOHN BARLEYCORN. Another pub noted for excellent food and service. Telephone: 01491 872509.

THE MILLER OF MANSFIELD HOTEL. The name comes from the story of the man who baked a pie for Henry II filled with illegal meat from one of the King's own deer. Telephone: 01491 872829.

EXLADE STREET

Length 5 miles

![Maharajah's Well, Stoke Row]

Maharajah's Well, Stoke Row

GETTING THERE: From Reading go over Caversham Bridge and turn left up the A4074 towards Wallingford. After 4 miles pass through Cane End, past the B4526 turning and then take your next right turn which is an unmarked road which forks off into the woods. This takes you into Exlade Street where you can park on the roadside around the Highwayman pub (please avoid parking in front of the houses or gateways). From Wallingford take the A4074 towards Caversham, and after 5 miles and climbing up the steep hill, turn left at the crossroads on top towards Checkendon. Take your first right after only a few yards and this leads you into Exlade Street where you park as listed above.

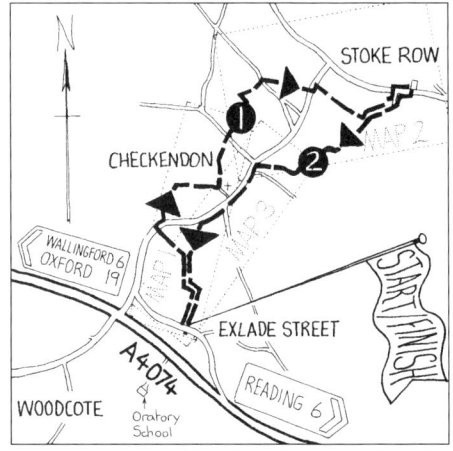

TERRAIN: Muddy in places particularly on bridleways. One gentle ascent, otherwise mainly flat.

START: (GR 659818) With your back to the Highwayman turn left and walk up the road 100 yards then turn right and go along the footpath up the left hand side of Mulberry Cottage.

MAP 1

INTRODUCTION: A wandering stroll through classic Chiltern countryside with isolated hamlets suddenly emerging from the woodland. There are timber-framed houses, a remote pub and an oriental well, while in between these is rolling pasture, mixed woodland and a park with geometrically perfect topiary!

EXLADE STREET: The first part of the name comes from 'slaed' meaning 'a valley' and the personal name 'Ecgi'. The second part is an 18th century addition from its position on the old Reading to Oxford road. The most notable buildings are the Highwayman pub which probably dates back to 1625 (but is rumoured to be 14th century in origin) and a 'crucks'-framed cottage nearby which is older still.

CHECKENDON COURT: A 16th century house in origin which was virtually rebuilt in 1920 in a Tudor style. The estate dates back to 1030 and a religious order is said to have lived on the site, with the present building still being visited by a spectral nun!

THE BLACK HORSE: A genuinely remote and unspoilt rural pub, which has been in the same family since 1952. It was first mentioned in 1779 but the building is older and was probably a staging post for those travelling on the Judges Road, a once important route from Oxford to Henley.

BASSET MANOR: This timber-framed house dates from the 16th century and was allegedly built on the site of a Norman hunting lodge. It was rebuilt in 1695 and has since been the home of Charles Reade, an author

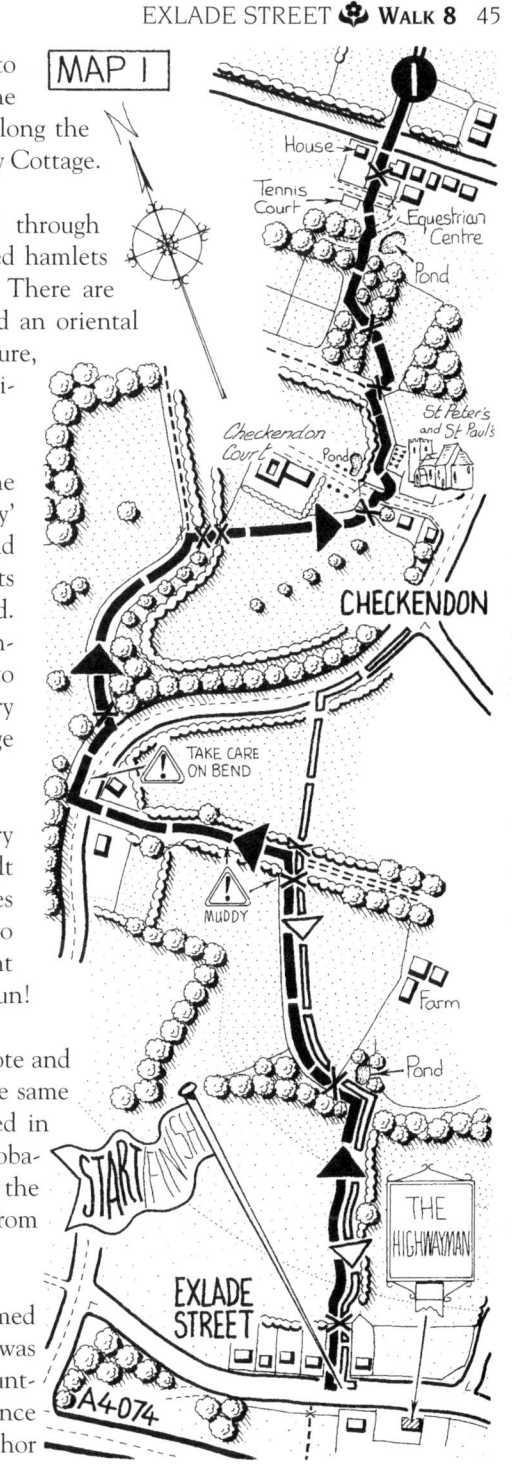

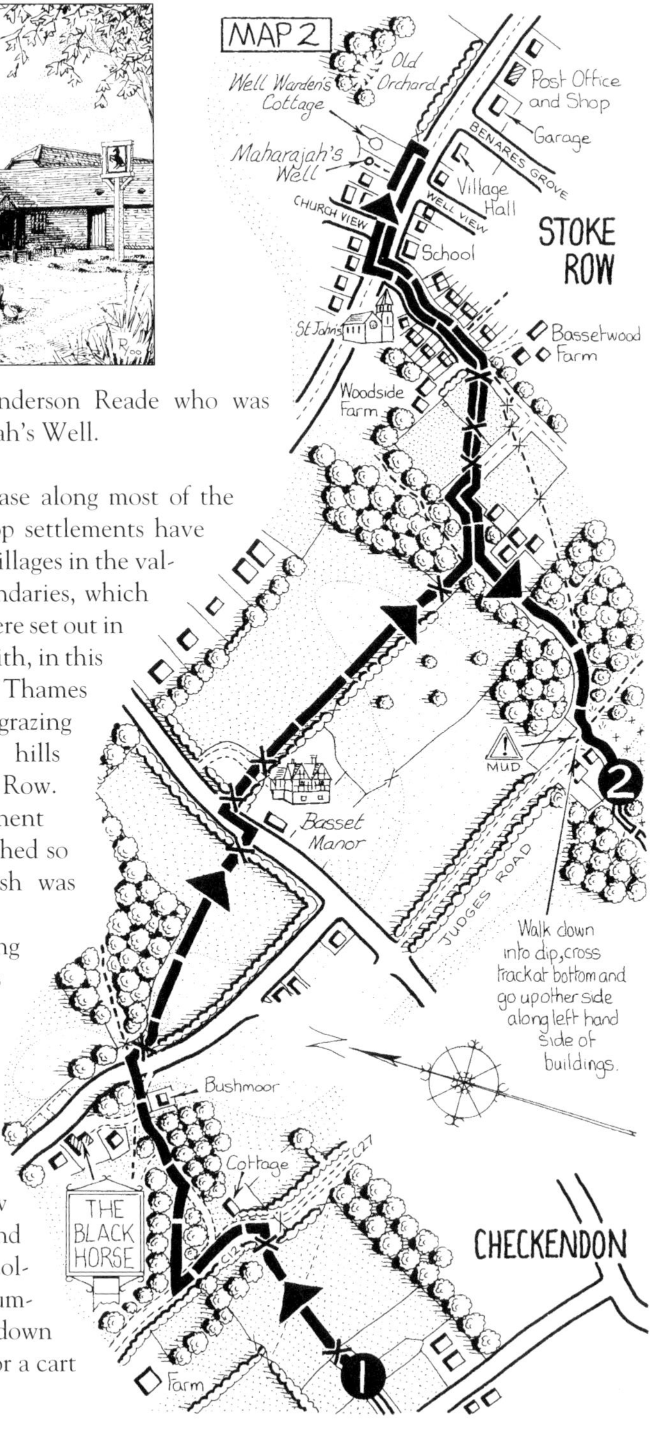

The Black Horse

and brother of Edward Anderson Reade who was responsible for the Maharajah's Well.

STOKE ROW: As is the case along most of the Chiltern escarpment, hilltop settlements have developed from associated villages in the valleys below. The parish boundaries, which date back to Saxon times, were set out in parallel strips up the slope with, in this case, North Stoke by the Thames having rights to timber and grazing in the woodland on the hills around what is now Stoke Row. Over the centuries permanent settlements became established so that by 1849 a new parish was formed here.

The biggest problem facing these hilltop villages was water supply. Ponds set in the thin clay and gravel layer which covers the porous chalk were the main source. Wells could be dug but with the water table more than 300 ft below the surface, this was risky and expensive. Rainwater was collected off roofs but in hot summers nothing short of going down to the valley with buckets or a cart would do.

MAP 2

Old Orchard

Well Warden's Cottage

Maharajah's Well

CHURCH VIEW

Post Office and Shop

Garage

BENARES GROVE

Village Hall

WELL VIEW

School

STOKE ROW

St Johns

Bassetwood Farm

Woodside Farm

Basset Manor

MUD

JUDGES ROAD

Walk down into dip, cross track at bottom and go up other side along left hand side of buildings.

Bushmoor

Cottage

CHECKENDON

THE BLACK HORSE

Farm

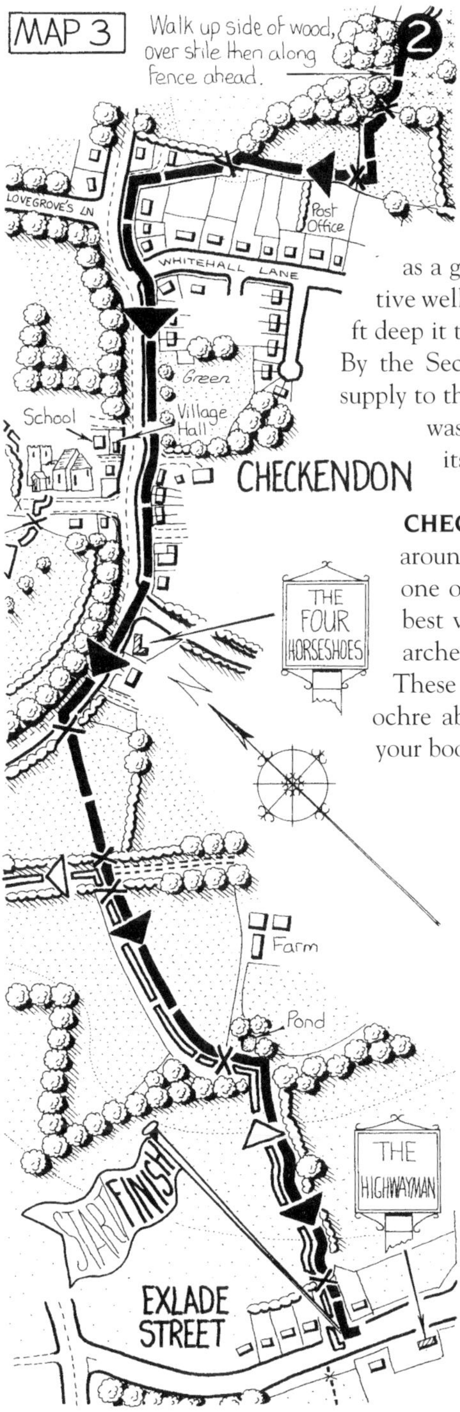

MAP 3

Walk up side of wood, over stile then along fence ahead.

LOVEGROVE'S LN

Post Office

WHITEHALL LANE

Green

School

Village Hall

CHECKENDON

THE FOUR HORSESHOES

Farm

Pond

START/FINISH

THE HIGHWAYMAN

EXLADE STREET

The Maharajah of Benares was surprised to hear of this plight when it was described to him by local resident Edward Anderson Reade while he was Governor of North West Provinces of India in the 1850s. Neither did he forget it, for when he wanted to thank Reade for his help during the Indian Mutiny the Maharajah gave sufficient funds as a gift to build a well at Stoke Row. The decorative well was opened in 1864 but at approximately 350 ft deep it took ten minutes to pull up a bucket of water! By the Second World War there was a reliable water supply to the village but the well was not forgotten for it was visited by the Duke of Edinburgh to celebrate its centenary.

CHECKENDON: A pretty collection of cottages around the church, St Peter and St Paul's, which is one of the oldest in the Chilterns. Its antiquity is best viewed from within where two large Norman arches lead the eye to the wall paintings in the apse. These are of the apostles and were painted in red ochre about 700-800 years ago! (Remember to take your boots off before entering.)

Fragments of 13th wall painting, Checkendon.

REFRESHMENTS:
THE HIGHWAYMAN. Ancient inn full of character, good food and beers! Open all day Saturday and Sunday. Telephone: 01491 682020.
THE BLACK HORSE. Popular walkers' pub with good beer (but only snacks). Telephone: 01491 680418.
THE FOUR HORSESHOES. Good, friendly local with thatched roof and large garden. Telephone: 01491 680325.

Walk 9
STANFORD DINGLEY
Length 5 miles

GETTING THERE: Stanford Dingley lies west of the A340 which links the A329 at Pangbourne with the A4 at Theale. Approaching from Reading head west on the A4, over junction 12 of the M4, around Theale and then turn right up the A340. Almost immediately take your first left and follow this road for 1½ miles then turn left to Bradfield Southend. On entering the village turn right by the Queen's Head pub and follow Cock Lane for 2 miles, past the Traveller's Rest, and down into Stanford Dingley. Carry on over the bridge, past the Bull and park next to the church (there is also some limited parking near the pubs).

TERRAIN: Two short, sharp climbs up to Tutts Clump then mainly flat. Muddy in places so go prepared.

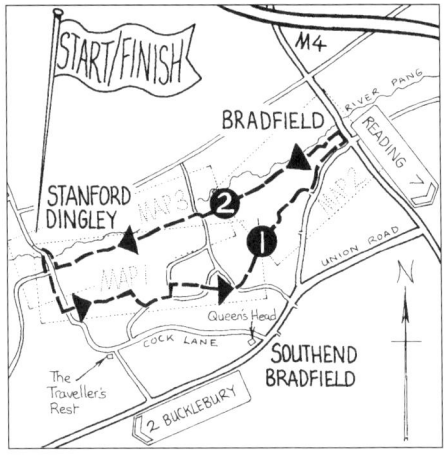

START: (GR 575716) From the church follow the road back into the village and then fork right opposite the Bull up the side of the small green. This takes you up to the front of the Old Mill, where you turn right

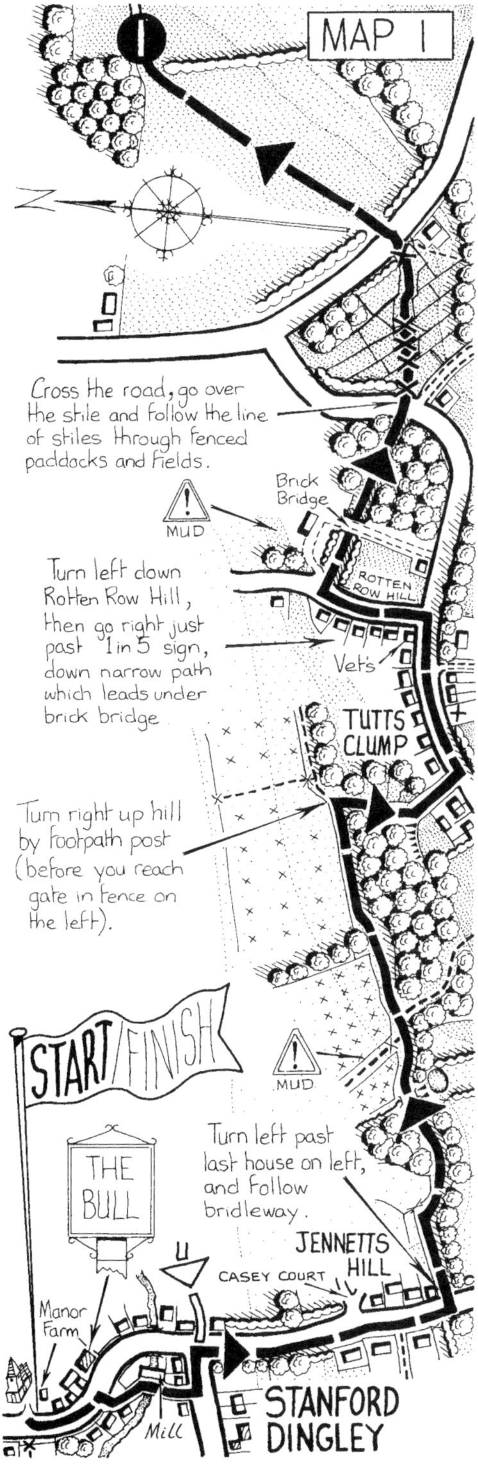

MAP 1

Cross the road, go over the stile and follow the line of stiles through fenced paddocks and fields.

⚠ MUD

Brick Bridge

Turn left down Rotten Row Hill, then go right just past 1 in 5 sign, down narrow path which leads under brick bridge.

ROTTEN ROW HILL

Vet's

TUTTS CLUMP

Turn right up hill by footpath post (before you reach gate in fence on the left).

START/FINISH

THE BULL

⚠ MUD

Turn left past last house on left, and follow bridleway.

JENNETTS HILL

CASEY COURT

Manor Farm

Mill

STANFORD DINGLEY

along a line of front doors, up the gravel drive and then turn left when you reach the road. Turn right at the T junction ahead and follow the road up and out of the village.

INTRODUCTION: Isolated in a network of narrow lanes, Stanford Dingley comprises a group of old brick houses astride the tree-lined River Pang, and despite the tiny size, it still supports two pubs. This journey meanders through woods, fields and isolated hamlets to Bradfield, which is dominated by the graceful Victorian college, and then returns along the picturesque river.

STANFORD DINGLEY: The image you may conjure up in your head at the mention of the rather quaint name of Stanford Dingley will probably be fairly close to its actual setting. An old mill straddling the river, timber-framed and brick cottages with picket-fenced gardens, two ancient pubs and a neat weatherboarded church. The lat-

St Deny's, Stanford Dingley.

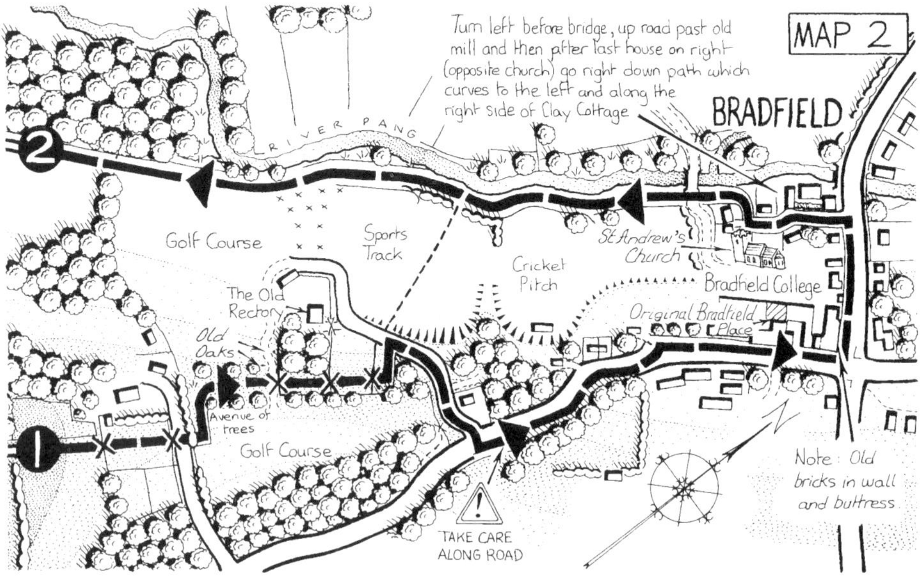

Turn left before bridge, up road past old mill and then after last house on right (opposite church) go right down path which curves to the left and along the right side of Clay Cottage

MAP 2

BRADFIELD

R I V E R   P A N G

Golf Course

Sports Track

St Andrew's Church

Cricket Pitch

Bradfield College

The Old Rectory

Original Bradfield Place

Old Oaks

Avenue of trees

Golf Course

Note: Old bricks in wall and buttress.

⚠ TAKE CARE ALONG ROAD

ter has the rare dedication to St Denys, a 3rd century French martyr who after being beheaded, so legend has it, picked up his severed appendage and walked off with it. Eventually he put his head down and on this spot he was buried. The image of the headless saint was popular in medieval art and appears on the lectern in this church.

THE OLD RECTORY (Bradfield): Rebuilt in 1882 after Thomas Stevens left it in rather a poor state, it is now surrounded by a golf course and sports fields! As you walk above it look out for some ancient oaks which predate all that surrounds them.

BRADFIELD: The village you see today was mostly the creation of a Victorian rector, Thomas Stevens, whose endless enthusiasm for many a great project was only blighted by his lack of financial reasoning!

Bradfield was first recorded 1,200 years before Stevens' time, in a Saxon document which implies that there may have been a short-lived monastic site here! There cer-

tainly was an old mansion here, Bradfield Place, which Stevens inherited and then incorporated into his college. (A stone buttress and brick wall of a 190 ft barn associated with the old house has been built into the current building, beside the crossroads.)

Thomas was the second son of Bradfield's Rector and Squire, Henry Stevens, and after the premature death of his elder brother the family encouraged him to be ordained. He was so in 1839 and became Rector when his father passed away in 1842. Stevens set about not only restoring but greatly enlarging the humble parish church, only to find

REFRESHMENTS:

THE OLD BOOT INN. A 250 year old pub said to be haunted by a man who hung himself in the orchard! Today, thankfully, you are far more likely to receive a warm welcome and good food and beer. Telephone: 0118 974 5213.
THE BULL. Even older pub famed for the Ring the Bull game where you have to swing a ring over a bull's horn! Good value food and beer. Closed on Mondays. Telephone: 0118 974 4409.

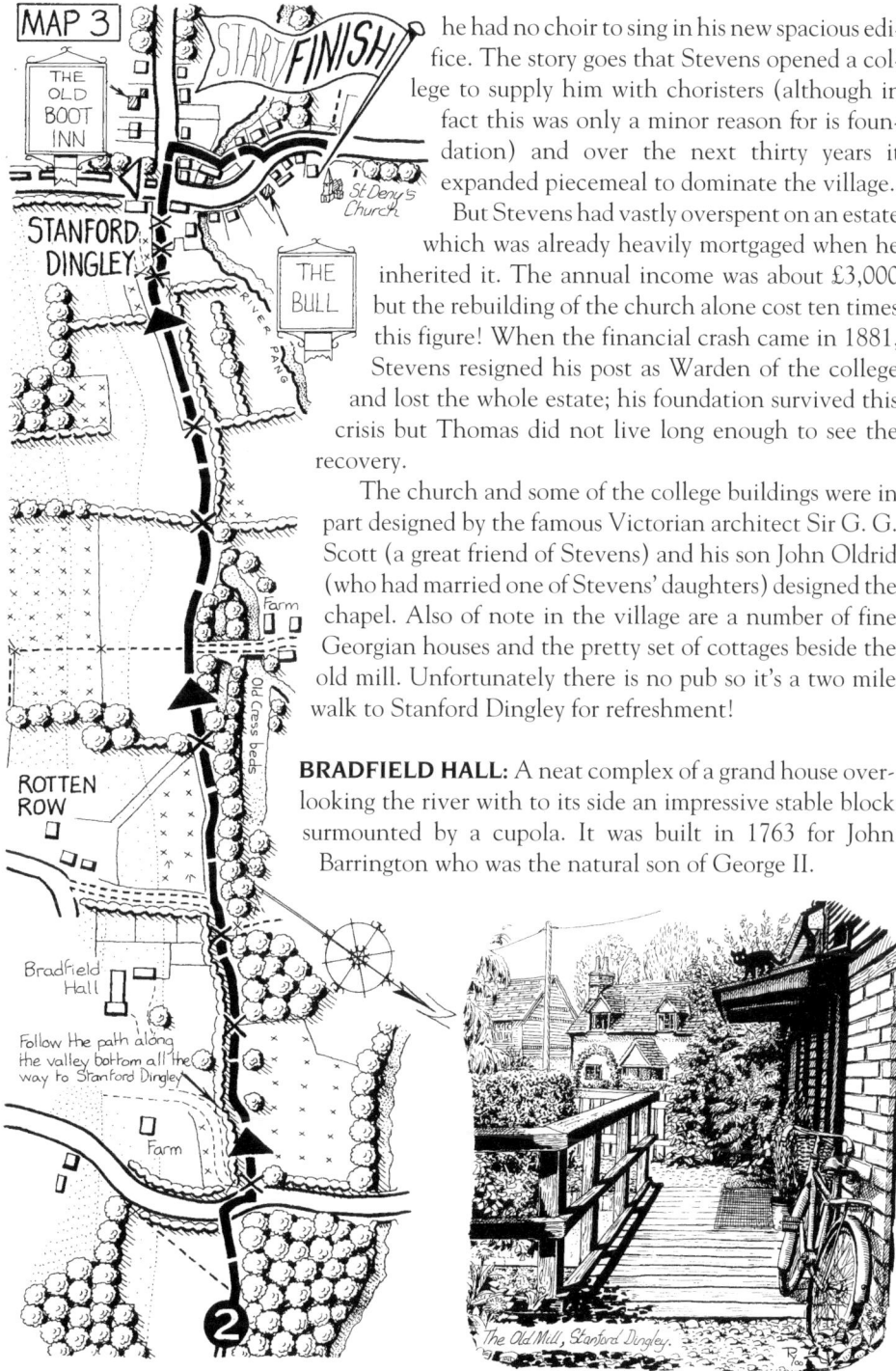

MAP 3

START/FINISH

THE
OLD
BOOT
INN

St Denys
Church

STANFORD
DINGLEY

THE
BULL

RIVER PANG

Farm

Old Cress beds

ROTTEN
ROW

Bradfield
Hall

Follow the path along
the valley bottom all the
way to Stanford Dingley

Farm

②

The Old Mill, Stanford Dingley.

he had no choir to sing in his new spacious edifice. The story goes that Stevens opened a college to supply him with choristers (although in fact this was only a minor reason for is foundation) and over the next thirty years it expanded piecemeal to dominate the village.

But Stevens had vastly overspent on an estate which was already heavily mortgaged when he inherited it. The annual income was about £3,000 but the rebuilding of the church alone cost ten times this figure! When the financial crash came in 1881, Stevens resigned his post as Warden of the college and lost the whole estate; his foundation survived this crisis but Thomas did not live long enough to see the recovery.

The church and some of the college buildings were in part designed by the famous Victorian architect Sir G. G. Scott (a great friend of Stevens) and his son John Oldrid (who had married one of Stevens' daughters) designed the chapel. Also of note in the village are a number of fine Georgian houses and the pretty set of cottages beside the old mill. Unfortunately there is no pub so it's a two mile walk to Stanford Dingley for refreshment!

BRADFIELD HALL: A neat complex of a grand house overlooking the river with to its side an impressive stable block surmounted by a cupola. It was built in 1763 for John Barrington who was the natural son of George II.

COLLINS END
Length 3¾ miles

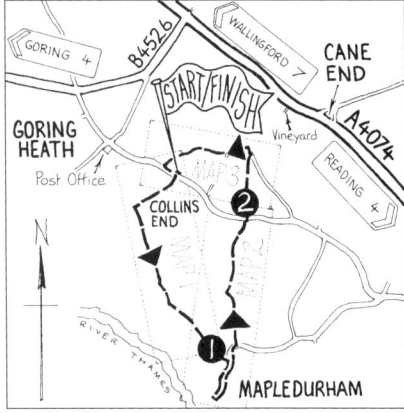

View over Mapledurham

GETTING THERE: Collins End is situated to the south of the A4074 between Reading and Wallingford. Approaching from Reading go over Caversham Bridge and turn left up the A4074. After 4 miles pass through Cane End, past the vineyard and then turn left down the B4526 towards Goring. Take the first left turn as the road bends to the right and follow this narrow road up to the crossroads, where you turn left. The King Charles Head is on the left in the wood, and there is parking along the right hand side of the road.

TERRAIN: One steep climb (but take your time and enjoy the view!) and one gentle one. Muddy in places through the woods.

START: (GR 664788) Cross over the stile in the hedge on the opposite side of the road from the pub into a small triangular field. Go across it and through the gap to the right of the far corner. Almost immediately turn right over a stile in a short fence (ignoring

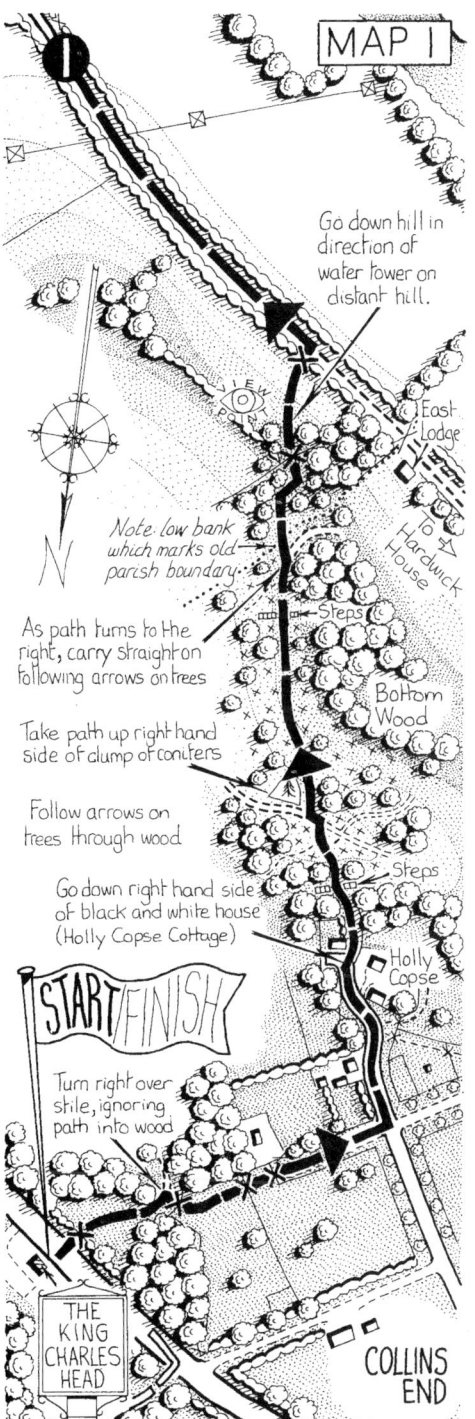

MAP 1

Go down hill in direction of water tower on distant hill.

East Lodge

To Hardwick House

Note: low bank which marks old parish boundary.

As path turns to the right, carry straight on following arrows on trees

Steps

Take path up right hand side of clump of conifers

Bottom Wood

Follow arrows on trees through wood

Go down right hand side of black and white house (Holly Copse Cottage)

Steps

Holly Copse

START/FINISH

Turn right over stile, ignoring path into wood

THE KING CHARLES HEAD

COLLINS END

the path continuing round the left into the wood) and walk along the hedge on your left in the next field.

INTRODUCTION: What a pleasant surprise it comes as you drive along this anonymous country lane to find, standing alone and surrounded by imposing beechwoods, the King Charles Head pub. This isolation, in their case of a religious nature, was shared by the Catholic Blount family whose home of Mapledurham is at the other end of this walk. Above their Thames-side idyll is a countryside of fields, heathland and tree clad hills which command excellent views over the peaceful river.

COLLINS END: A small hamlet at the southern end of Goring Heath. Goring Heath is notable for the almshouses (just north of the former post office which itself is a picturesque building of 1900) which were founded for Henry Alnutt, the Lord Mayor of London, in 1724.

BOTTOM WOOD: Classic Chiltern beechwood where felling has broken the usual monotony by attracting new flora and giving the remaining trees dramatic space. Look out for an innocuous bank and ditch just before you leave the wood, which as it marks the parish boundary between Hardwick and Mapledurham may be of some antiquity.

HARDWICK HOUSE: Built in the 16th century by the Lybbe family who had purchased the manor in 1526 from the Hardwicks. Elizabeth I is said to have stayed here in the medallioned bedroom which still bears her name. The estate was bought by Sir Charles Day Rose in the 19th century and it is his emblem of a rose which you can see on the gates by the East Lodge.

Mapledurham Mill.

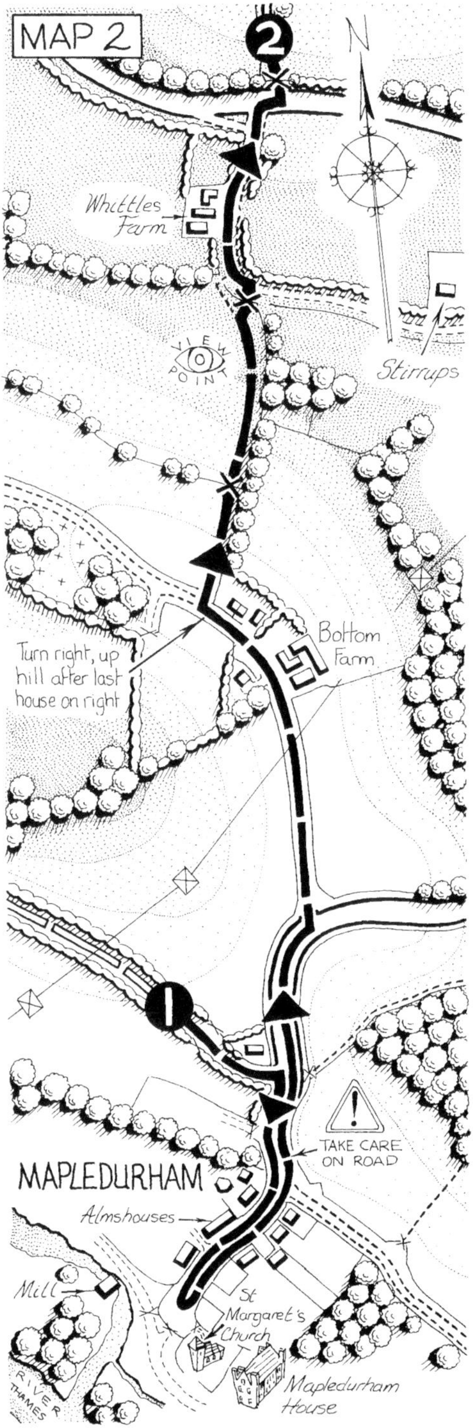

MAPLEDURHAM HOUSE: This large Tudor red brick mansion was built from 1588 by Sir Michael Blount to replace the old timber-framed house, a part of which survives as an outbuilding. His descendants were staunch Catholics and the house has relics of their turbulent existence with priest's holes, trap doors and remains of secret passages! Eventually in 1789 they were permitted to build a Catholic chapel but even then this was on the special condition that the exterior was made to look like the adjacent servants' quarters, so as not to attract public attention!

The house featured in the final chapters of *The Forsyte Saga* and its guests have included Elizabeth I and the 18th century poet Alexander Pope.

Pope was charmed by the Blount sisters Martha and Teresa and spent much time at Mapledurham, eventually pronouncing his love to the younger Martha. Pope's hunch-backed demeanour, due to childhood tuber-culosis of the spine, probably didn't make him such an attractive proposition and their relationships were soured after this event. Despite this he left £1,000 and three score of his books to Martha in his will. The house is privately owned but is open to the public from Easter until the end of September, Saturday, Sunday and bank holidays, 2 pm to 5 pm.

MAP 2

N

Whittles Farm

VIEW POINT

Stirrups

Bottom Farm

Turn right, up hill after last house on right

MAPLEDURHAM

Almshouses

Mill

St Margaret's Church

TAKE CARE ON ROAD

Mapledurham House

RIVER THAMES

MAPLEDURHAM: A beautiful collection of brick houses, mainly built to serve the estate. The White House was once the village pub called the Kings Arms but it was closed by the Lord of the Manor due to 'excessive conviviality on the Sabbath'! One of the oldest buildings is the row of single-storey almshouses built in 1614 by Richard Blount. The most picturesque is the mill, which is the only working one left on the Thames, yet its timber-framed core dates back to the 16th century.

St Margaret's church opposite has a chapel on the south side which was used by the Catholic Blount family despite the rest of the church being Protestant. This inevitably led the incumbent Church of England vicars to try to remove the family's rights to the chapel, including an attempt by one Rev Lord Augustus Fitz-Clarence. He is notable as being one of the ten children of King William IV and his mistress Mrs Jordan, and the King's influence was used to land Augustus the post at Mapledurham. The previous vicar was the unambitious John Bird Sumner who suddenly in 1828 found himself promoted 'at the urgent insistance of the Crown' (sic) to the position of Bishop of Chester! Despite the dubious means with which Augustus became vicar he seems to have been respected by the villagers and is buried in the churchyard.

Another memorial at St Margaret's is to Sir Charles Day Rose (see Hardwick House) who 'died April 20th 1913 from the effects of an aeroplane flight'.

NUNEY GREEN: A tiny woodland hamlet whose residents had to walk all the way to Mapledurham to worship. The route you take past Whittles Farm and through Nuney Wood is the same as they had to walk and is known as Church Way.

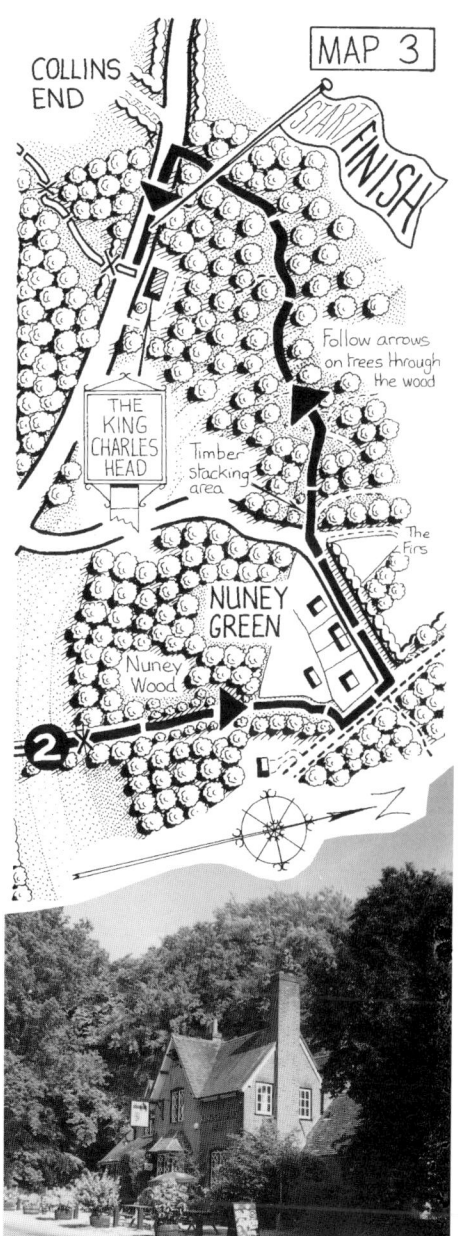

The King Charles Head pub.

REFRESHMENTS:
THE KING CHARLES HEAD. Excellent food and beers. Telephone: 01491 680268.

Walk 11
SONNING
Length 5½ miles

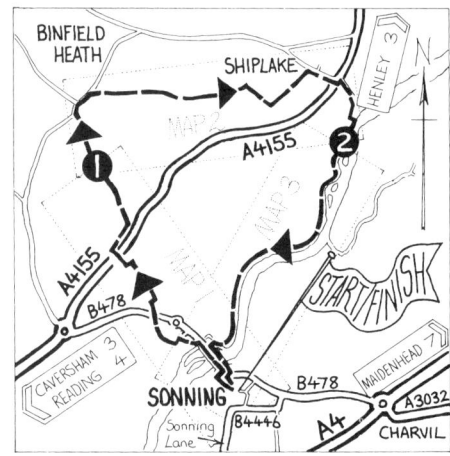

Sonning Bridge

GETTING THERE: Sonning can be reached from two turnings off the A4 between Reading and Maidenhead. Approaching from Reading pass over the railway and turn left into Sonning Lane (B4446). On entering the village you can park on the left alongside the wall, or carry on around the bend and take your first left into High Street. This leads down to a left hand turn by the Bull Inn and there is further parking alongside the wall up the hill.

MOORING: On the towpath side below Sonning Lock. Walk up past the lock and join the walk at Sonning Bridge.

TERRAIN: One steady climb up to Binfield Heath. Be prepared for mud in some of the fields.

START: (GR 756755) From the courtyard at the front of the Bull Inn go through the gate into the churchyard and follow the left hand of the two paths up to the corner of

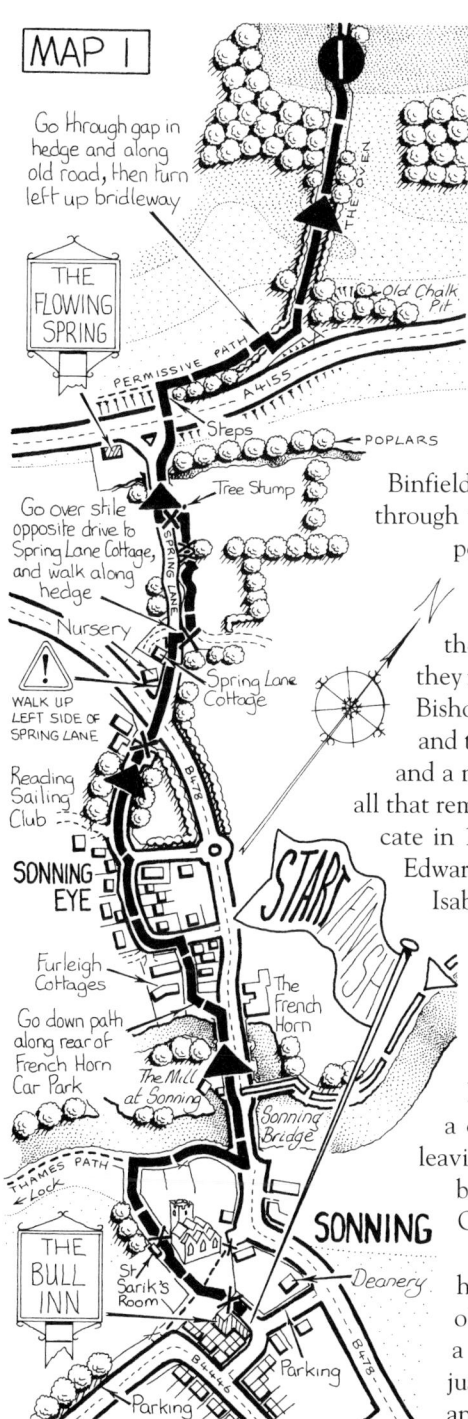

MAP 1

Go through gap in hedge and along old road, then turn left up bridleway

THE FLOWING SPRING

PERMISSIVE PATH

A4155

THE OVEN

Old Chalk Pit

Steps

POPLARS

Tree Stump

Go over stile opposite drive to Spring Lane Cottage, and walk along hedge

Nursery

⚠ WALK UP LEFT SIDE OF SPRING LANE

Spring Lane Cottage

SPRING LANE

B478

Reading Sailing Club

SONNING EYE

Furleigh Cottages

Go down path along rear of French Horn Car Park

The Mill at Sonning

START

The French Horn

Sonning Bridge

THAMES PATH Lock

THE BULL INN

St Sarik's Room

SONNING

Deanery

Parking

B478

Parking

the old wall and then between it and the church. Go around the right side of St Sarik's Room and continue along the path behind it.

If you parked back on Sonning Lane then go up to the corner and along the path to the left of Turpins which leads into the churchyard. Turn left at the end of the wall and follow the route past St Sarik's Room.

INTRODUCTION: The starting point of this walk is one of the most attractive Thames-side villages, resplendent with its narrow red brick bridge, ancient high walls and rustic cottages. From here you visit the little Gothic chapel at Binfield Heath, then historic Shiplake and return through the reeds, woods and meadows which line this peaceful length of the Thames.

SONNING: This now wayside village was once the seat of the Saxon Bishops of Ramsbury until they relocated to Old Sarum in the 11th century. The Bishops retained a palace here until the 16th century and the old wall you walk along south of the church and a mound on your left as you approach the river is all that remains of it. When Richard II was forced to abdicate in 1399 (the only other English monarch besides Edward VIII to take this action) his 12 year old wife Isabella took refuge with the Bishop at Sonning. Her ghost is said to haunt the riverside although she died elsewhere after marrying for a second time. Another historic character connected with Sonning is Dick Turpin, whose aunt owned the cottage on the corner of Sonning Lane (now called Turpins). He allegedly robbed a coach on Bath Road and then galloped here, leaving Black Bess in secret stables at the cottage before running to safety over the bridge into Oxfordshire!

The humble bridge looks older than it is, having been built in the 18th century, while the old mill next to it was closed in 1969 and is now a restaurant and theatre. Also of note is Deanery, just north of the Bull Inn and hidden behind the ancient tall walls which the architect Sir Edwin

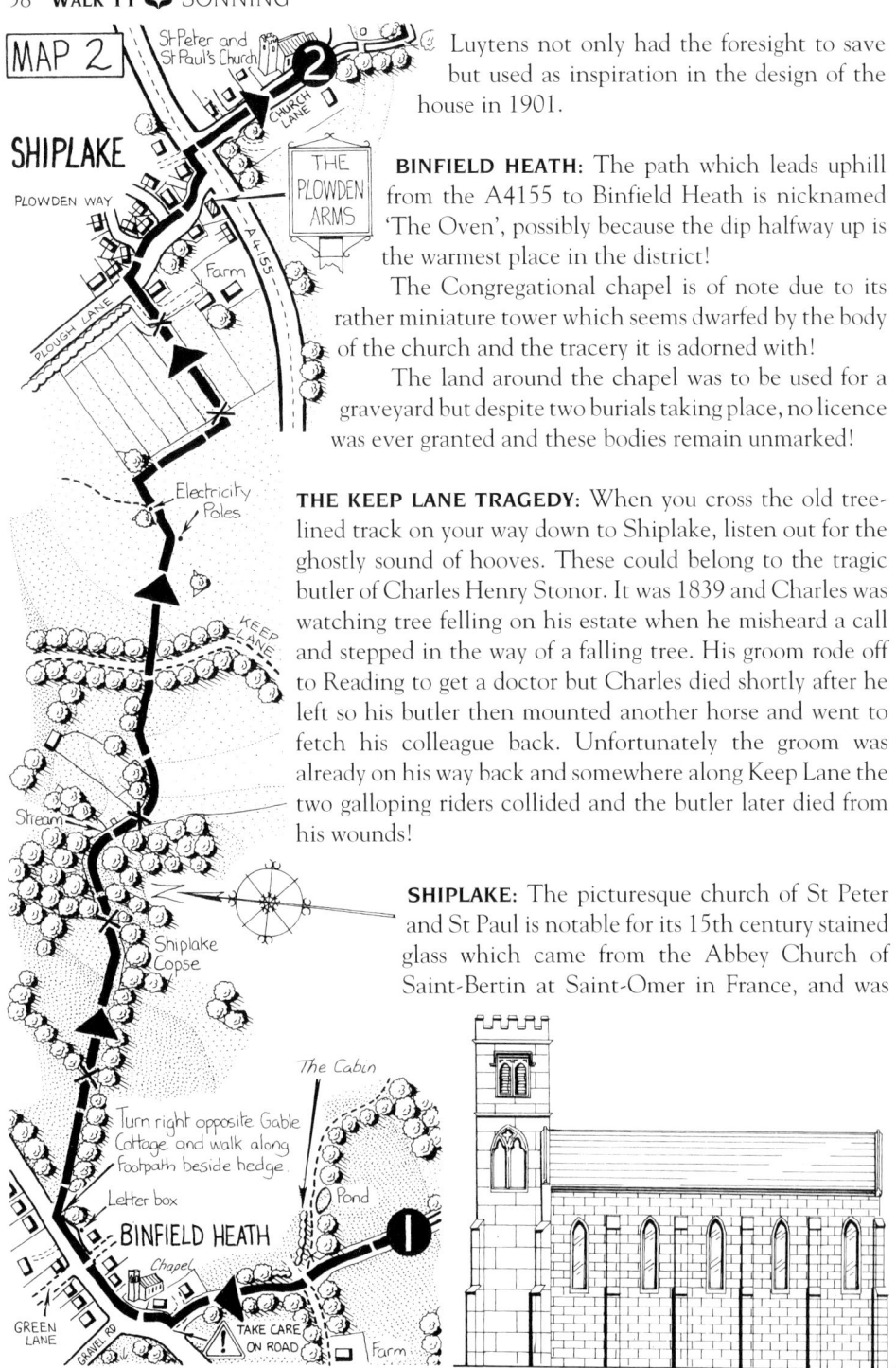

MAP 2

SHIPLAKE

St Peter and St Paul's Church

PLOWDEN WAY

CHURCH LANE

THE PLOWDEN ARMS

PLOUGH LANE

Farm

A4155

Electricity Poles

KEEP LANE

Stream

Shiplake Copse

The Cabin

Turn right opposite Gable Cottage and walk along footpath beside hedge.

Pond

Letter box

BINFIELD HEATH

Chapel

GREEN LANE

GRAVEL RD

TAKE CARE ON ROAD

Farm

Luytens not only had the foresight to save but used as inspiration in the design of the house in 1901.

BINFIELD HEATH: The path which leads uphill from the A4155 to Binfield Heath is nicknamed 'The Oven', possibly because the dip halfway up is the warmest place in the district!

The Congregational chapel is of note due to its rather miniature tower which seems dwarfed by the body of the church and the tracery it is adorned with!

The land around the chapel was to be used for a graveyard but despite two burials taking place, no licence was ever granted and these bodies remain unmarked!

THE KEEP LANE TRAGEDY: When you cross the old tree-lined track on your way down to Shiplake, listen out for the ghostly sound of hooves. These could belong to the tragic butler of Charles Henry Stonor. It was 1839 and Charles was watching tree felling on his estate when he misheard a call and stepped in the way of a falling tree. His groom rode off to Reading to get a doctor but Charles died shortly after he left so his butler then mounted another horse and went to fetch his colleague back. Unfortunately the groom was already on his way back and somewhere along Keep Lane the two galloping riders collided and the butler later died from his wounds!

SHIPLAKE: The picturesque church of St Peter and St Paul is notable for its 15th century stained glass which came from the Abbey Church of Saint-Bertin at Saint-Omer in France, and was

Binfield Heath Congregational Chapel.

presented to the church in 1830. The church was also where Alfred Lord Tennyson was married in 1850. He stayed at the Old Vicarage and even referred to it in verse as the vicarage by the quarry

(this is the chalk pit you pass before the boathouses). Behind the church is Shiplake Court built in 1905, used by the BBC in World War II and now a college. The previous house on the site had been demolished in 1804 after it had been sold by the extravagant Henry Constantine Jennings.

He inherited the family home which had been purchased from the Plowdens in 1689 (hence the nearby pub is called the Plowden Arms), but during travels in Europe he started a fateful habit of collecting artefacts. Yet he was already in great debt, leading him to rent out Shiplake Court and having his first son born in a hotel! After his first wife died he remarried when he convinced a 17 year old heiress to run away with him, but in 1777 he was arrested and again in 1783, this time ending up in prison due to gambling debts. He bought his freedom in 1791 with money left to him upon his mother's death, but he retained some odd habits from his time in jail, being known to swing a mock sword 300 times in the morning and drilling every evening before bed! He sold Shiplake in 1801 to repay even more debts and died in 1819 after spending more time in prison and having amassed 21 lawsuits during his colourful life!

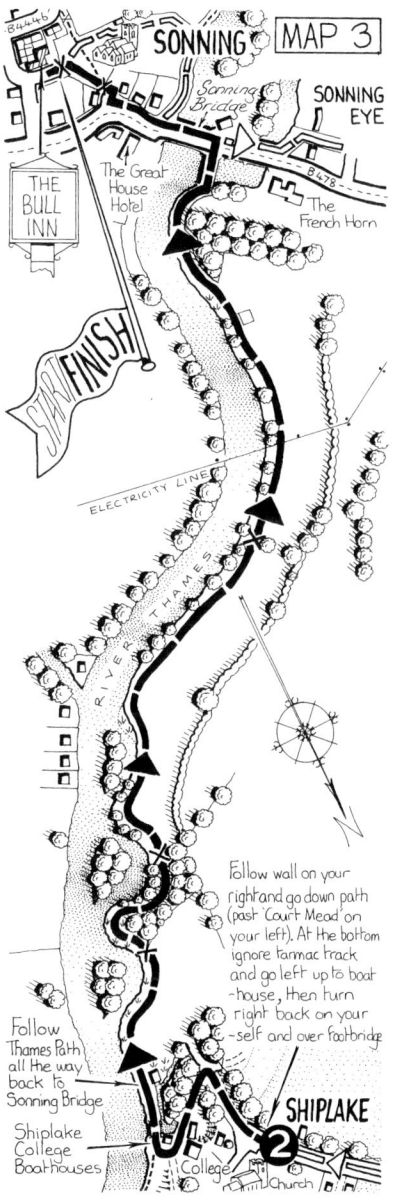

REFRESHMENTS:

THE BULL INN. Wisteria clad timber-framed building, which is atmospheric inside and out. Imaginative home made food and good beers on offer. Open all day Saturday and Sunday in summer. Telephone: 0118 969 3901.

THE FLOWING SPRING. A large pub by the A4155. Telephone: 0118 969 3207.

THE PLOWDEN ARMS. Another smart pub by the A4155. Telephone: 0118 940 2794. (Please note no food Sunday evening or all day Monday.)

Walk 12
WALTHAM ST LAWRENCE
Length 4¾ miles

The Bell, Waltham St Lawrence.

GETTING THERE: From Reading take the A4 towards Maidenhead, out of the town for about 6 miles and just after entering Hare Hatch take the right turn beside the Horse and Groom pub to Waltham. Go over the railway, enter the village and then park around the area of the Bell. From Maidenhead take the A4 towards Reading and then just before the A404(M) turn left towards White Waltham. Follow this road for 4 miles through White Waltham and then just past the Star pub (on the B3024) turn right up The Street and park by the Bell.

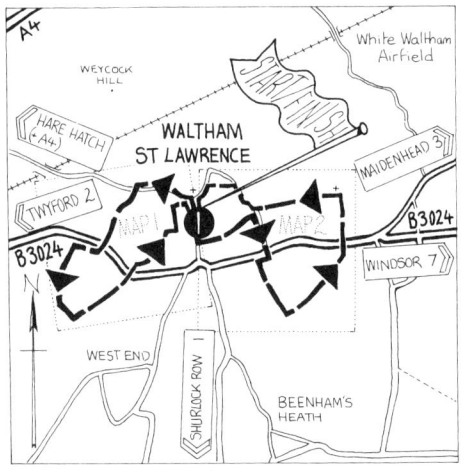

TERRAIN: Flat, with some boggy areas.

START: (GR 829769) With your back to the Bell head up Milley Road in front of you, past Neville Close and along the road (left hand side may be best).

SHORT CUT: This figure of eight route can be split into two separate walks. The eastern section is 2 miles while the western section is 2¾ miles.

trim meadows, and tree-lined lanes before returning via Shottesbrooke Park with its majestic spired church.

WALTHAM ST LAWRENCE: The name Waltham is believed to mean woodland (weald) enclosure (ham), a fact which is made more likely as it was known to be a Saxon royal estate within

MAP 1

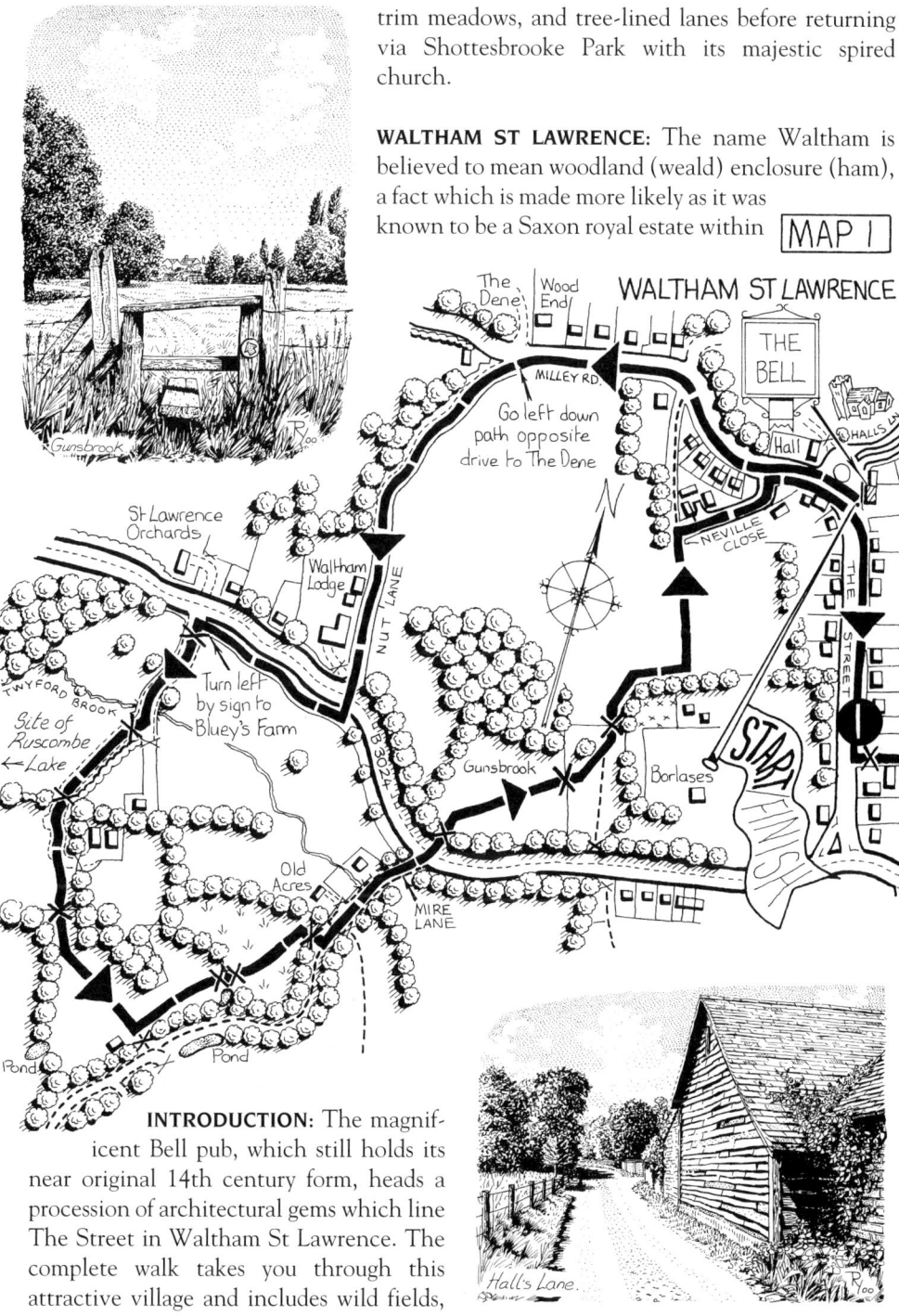

WALTHAM ST LAWRENCE

The Dene Wood End

MILLEY RD.

Go left down path opposite drive to The Dene

THE BELL

Hall

HALLS LN.

NEVILLE CLOSE

THE STREET

St Lawrence Orchards

Waltham Lodge

NUT LANE

B 3024

TWYFORD BROOK

Site of Ruscombe Lake

Turn left by sign to Bluey's Farm

Gunsbrook

Borlases

START

FINISH

Old Acres

MIRE LANE

Pond

Pond

Gunsbrook

Hall's Lane.

INTRODUCTION: The magnificent Bell pub, which still holds its near original 14th century form, heads a procession of architectural gems which line The Street in Waltham St Lawrence. The complete walk takes you through this attractive village and includes wild fields,

the Forest of Windsor. Another interpretation of the name is 'ill built', a description which could not be levelled at the present buildings in Waltham. The Bell is a timber-framed structure (appropriately of a design known as a Wealden house) which has stood for more than 600 years! The church opposite has Norman elements within its nave and the majority of the houses which line The Street date from the 15th-18th centuries.

Yet the Saxon Lords were not the first settlers here. Just to the north on Weycock Hill the remains of what has been described as a Roman temple were found and the area was likely to have been on the road from Silchester (south of Reading) to Verulanium (St Albans).

The most notable later residents from Waltham appear to be the Newberys, a local family who had great success in the publishing business. Thomas Newbery is credited with producing the first children's book in 1563, while Ralph Newbery became the Master of the Printing House to Queen Elizabeth I, and bequeathed the building which is now the Bell to the poor of the village in 1633. The most famous Newbery was John, who produced little children's books at St Paul's Churchyard in London and employed such notables of the 18th century as Dr Johnson and Oliver Goldsmith! He became known as Honest John and probably created 'Goody Two Shoes'. A medal for children's literature still bears his name.

RUSCOMBE LAKE: To the west of Waltham the Twyford Brook runs through a flat oval area before flowing down into the Loddon at Twyford. This spot was known as Ruscombe Lake (although it is unclear whether it was anything more than a marshy landscape before it was drained in the 19th century).

SHOTTESBROOKE PARK: Sotesbroc, as it was recorded in the Domesday Book, was held by Alward the Goldsmith and it is assumed that the precious metal was worked here. Later in 1335 Sir William Trussell of Staffordshire founded a college on the site (for six priests) and set about knocking down the old church and building a completely new edifice. His new church is notable as it is almost totally of this one period, and its dramatic proportions have not been diluted by later changes or additions. The architect certainly seemed pleased with his work as it is said he climbed the spire to toast the completion of the work only to topple off and fall to his death. He allegedly was buried at the spot where he fell!

As it was a religious foundation the college was dissolved by Henry VIII and its

St John the Baptist church, Shottesbrooke.

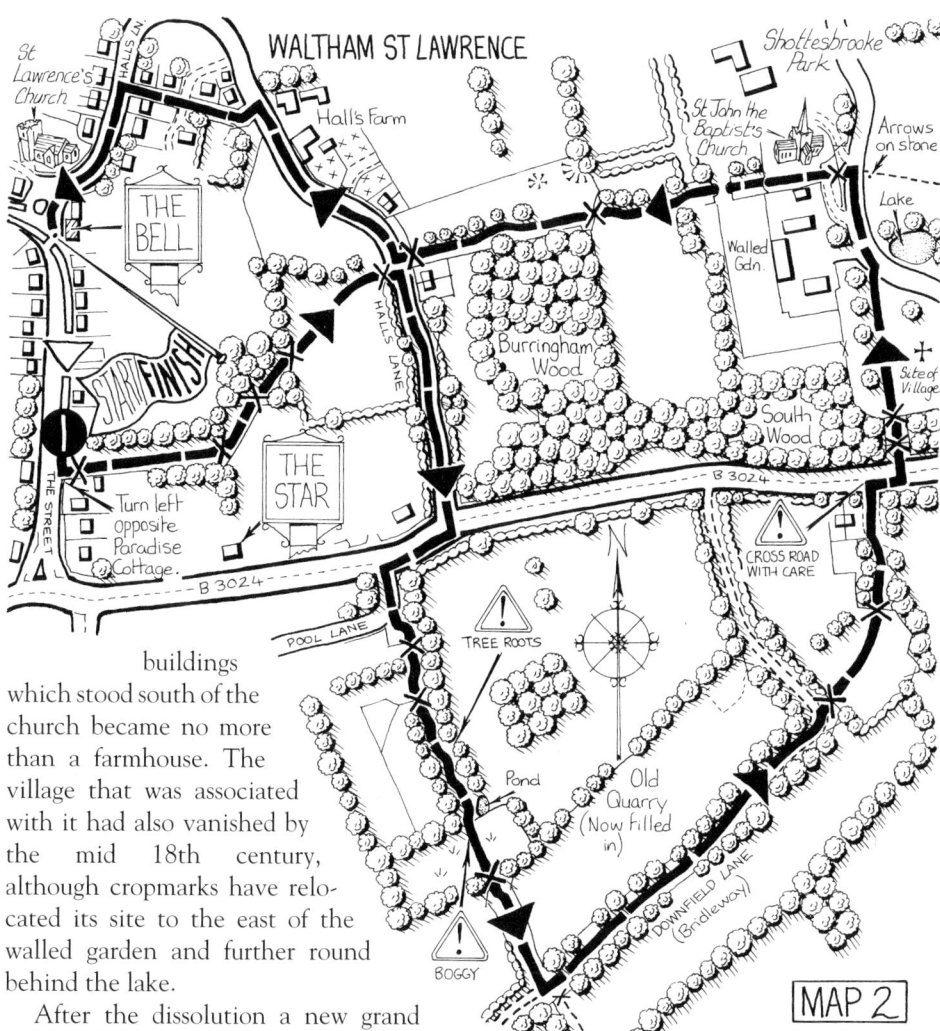

MAP 2

buildings which stood south of the church became no more than a farmhouse. The village that was associated with it had also vanished by the mid 18th century, although cropmarks have relocated its site to the east of the walled garden and further round behind the lake.

After the dissolution a new grand house, Shottesbrooke Park, was built north of the church. Its most notable incumbent was Francis Cherry, who was a renowned Jacobite, that is one who remained loyal to the Stuart dynasty (from the Latin word 'Jacobus' meaning James). The Stuarts had been ousted by the Glorious Revolution of 1688 when the Protestant William of Orange was invited to take the throne as William III. Cherry is alleged to have tried to kill the new King one day while hunting. He noticed that William was staying close

to him as they rode so he led him on purpose over a dangerous jump, but without success.

REFRESHMENTS:

THE BELL. As attractive inside as it is out with good bar food to complement the well-kept beers. Telephone: 0118 934 1788.

THE STAR INN. Large pub on the B3024 which is a good alternative if the Bell is busy. Telephone: 0118 934 3486.

Walk 13
ROTHERFIELD GREYS
Length 4 miles

Greys Court

GETTING THERE: Rotherfield Greys lies on an unclassified road west of Henley-on-Thames. From Henley town centre go up the Market Square, past the Town Hall and ascend Gravel Hill. Keep following the road for about 2 miles, go past the Greys Court turning and then as the road goes uphill and bends to the right take the left turning straight on. Turn left at the junction almost immediately after and ½ mile further on you enter Rotherfield Greys. Go round the sharp left bend and park on either side of the road opposite the church.

TERRAIN: As befitting the Chilterns there are four climbs but these are all short. Be prepared for mud in some parts of the walk even in summer.

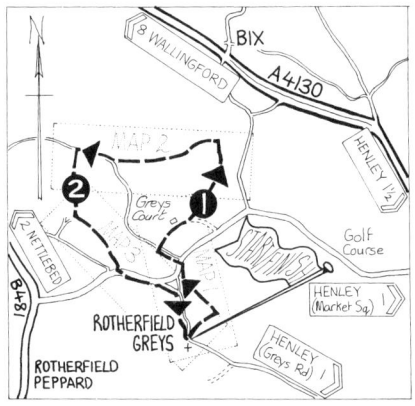

START: (GR 726823) With your back to the church, go through the gate between the bus shelter and the letter box. Take the left hand of the two paths offered and cross straight over the field and into the wood.

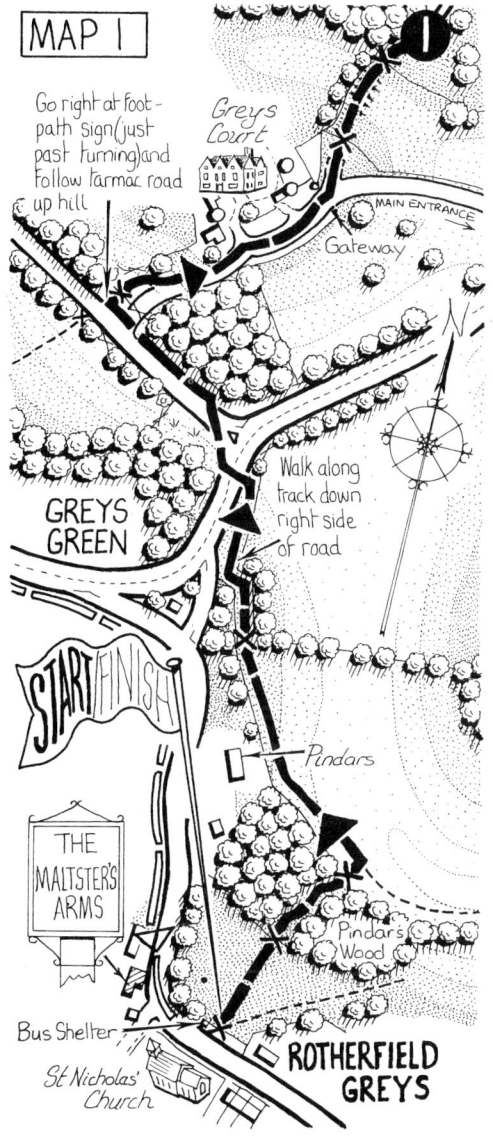

MAP 1

Go right at foot-path sign (just past turning) and follow tarmac road up hill

Greys Court

MAIN ENTRANCE

Gateway

N

Walk along track down right side of road

GREYS GREEN

START FINISH

Pindars

THE MALTSTER'S ARMS

Pindars Wood

Bus Shelter

St Nicholas' Church

ROTHERFIELD GREYS

The Old Keep, Greys Ct.

ROTHERFIELD GREYS: The rather odd name simply means 'field of an ox' with the name of the family who owned the manor added on later (eg Rotherfield Peppard belonged to the Peppard family). Once it was a more substantial settlement stretching towards Henley, but today just a few cottages line the road next to St Nicholas' church.

This humble edifice is worth a closer inspection as it contains the massive Knollys Monument. This colourful memorial to Sir Francis Knollys resembles a four (or in this case six) poster bed, decorated with cherubs, vases and statues. The two figures on top are his son William and his wife, who erected the chapel in 1605.

GREYS COURT: The Knollys were the most notorious owners of Greys Court which they were granted in 1514 by Henry VIII. At this time it was a fortified manor house surrounded by crenellated stone walls and

INTRODUCTION: Undulating valleys of grass manicured by sheep and beech woodland manipulated by man surround the rusticated, rather than grand, Greys Court. This walk not only includes a heavy dose of the above but returns along two 'picture postcard' greens and finishes at the equally picturesque Maltster's Arms.

REFRESHMENTS:
THE MALTSTER'S ARMS. Attractive white-washed old pub with a front seating area under the shade of a tree and a garden at the rear. Telephone: 01491 628400.

towers which had been built in around 1347 by the Lord de Grey. His family line ran out in 1387 and the next owners, the Lovells, lost the house to the Crown after the Battle of Bosworth.

The Knollys were an influential family in the court of Elizabeth I with Sir Francis marrying the Queen's cousin. Their daughter Lettice, on the other hand, was violently hated by Elizabeth after she had married the Queen's favourite, Lord Robert, Earl of Leicester, in 1578. Lettice was first married to Walter, Earl of Essex but while he was serving in Ireland she had started an affair with Leicester. Fortunately for her Essex died before he could return and when she discovered she was pregnant the Knollys forced Lord Robert into the marriage. When the Queen found out about the wedding she had Leicester locked up in the Tower and although she later forgave him, her contempt for his new wife never subsided.

It was Sir Francis who built the current

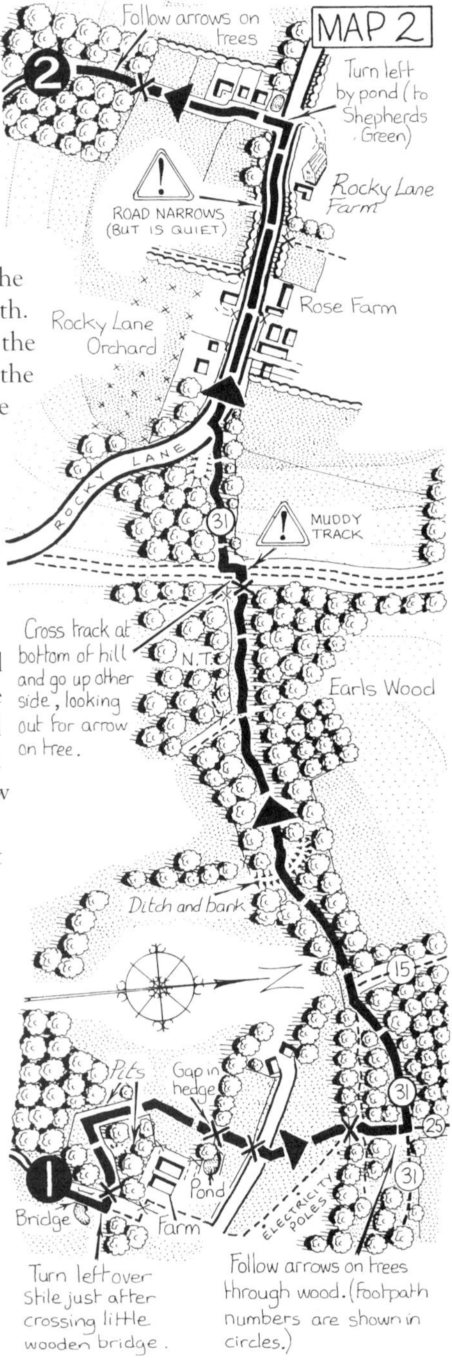

Rose Farm.

MAP 2

Follow arrows on trees

②

Turn left by pond (to Shepherds Green)

ROAD NARROWS (BUT IS QUIET)

Rocky Lane Farm

Rocky Lane Orchard

Rose Farm

ROCKY LANE

31

MUDDY TRACK

Cross track at bottom of hill and go up other side, looking out for arrow on tree.

N.T.

Earls Wood

Ditch and bank

15

Pits

Gap in hedge

31

25

1

Pond

Farm

31

Bridge

ELECTRICITY POLES

Turn left over stile just after crossing little wooden bridge.

Follow arrows on trees through wood. (Footpath numbers are shown in circles.)

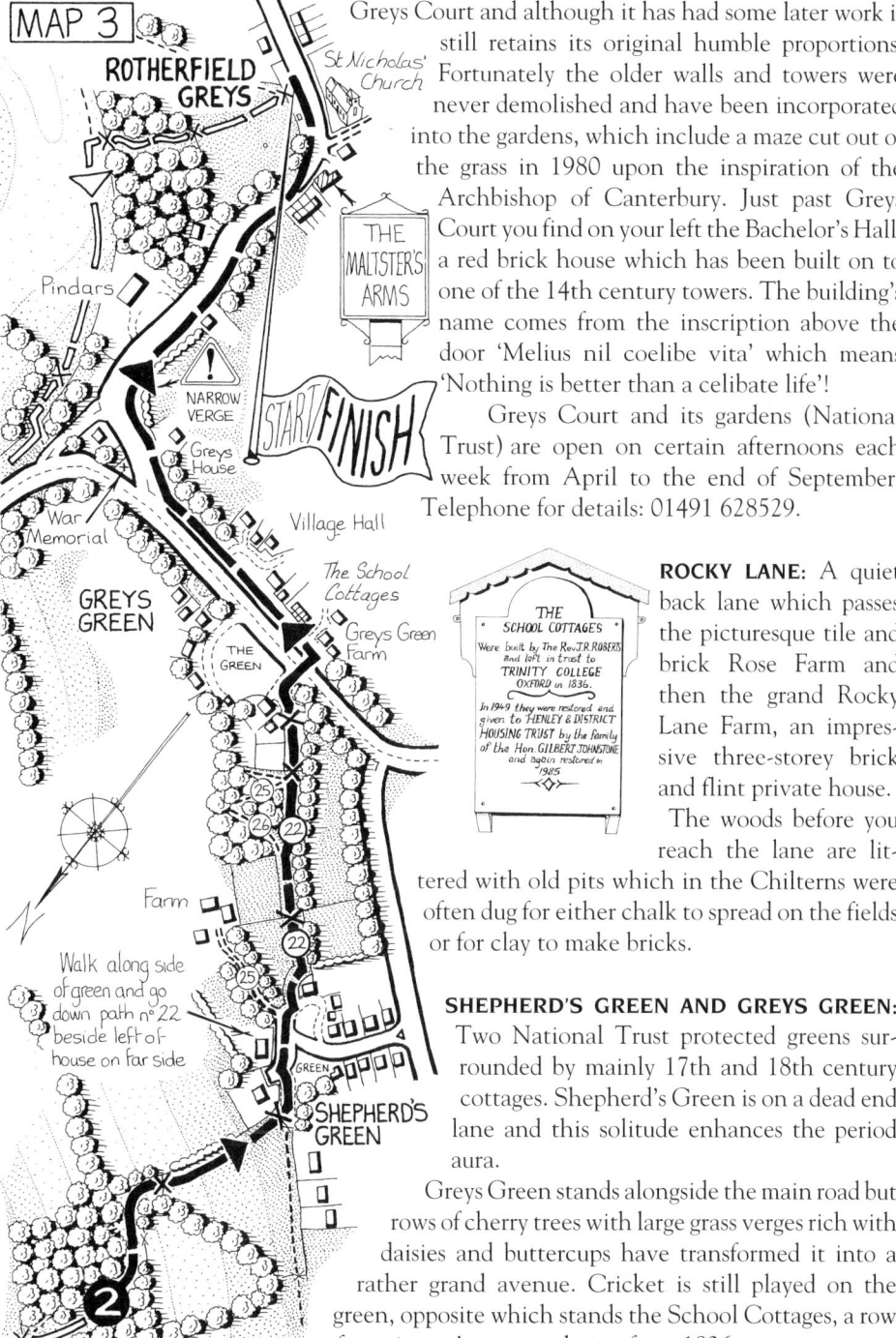

MAP 3

ROTHERFIELD GREYS

St Nicholas' Church

Pindars

THE MALTSTER'S ARMS

! NARROW VERGE

Greys House

START FINISH

War Memorial

Village Hall

GREYS GREEN

The School Cottages

Greys Green Farm

THE GREEN

25
26
22

Farm

Walk along side of green and go down path nº 22 beside left of house on far side

22

25

GREEN

SHEPHERD'S GREEN

2

THE SCHOOL COTTAGES

Were built by The Rev.J.R.ROBERTS and left in trust to TRINITY COLLEGE OXFORD in 1836.

In 1949 they were restored and given to HENLEY & DISTRICT HOUSING TRUST by the family of the Hon. GILBERT JOHNSTONE and again restored in 1985.

Greys Court and although it has had some later work it still retains its original humble proportions. Fortunately the older walls and towers were never demolished and have been incorporated into the gardens, which include a maze cut out of the grass in 1980 upon the inspiration of the Archbishop of Canterbury. Just past Greys Court you find on your left the Bachelor's Hall, a red brick house which has been built on to one of the 14th century towers. The building's name comes from the inscription above the door 'Melius nil coelibe vita' which means 'Nothing is better than a celibate life'!

Greys Court and its gardens (National Trust) are open on certain afternoons each week from April to the end of September. Telephone for details: 01491 628529.

ROCKY LANE: A quiet back lane which passes the picturesque tile and brick Rose Farm and then the grand Rocky Lane Farm, an impressive three-storey brick and flint private house.

The woods before you reach the lane are littered with old pits which in the Chilterns were often dug for either chalk to spread on the fields or for clay to make bricks.

SHEPHERD'S GREEN AND GREYS GREEN: Two National Trust protected greens surrounded by mainly 17th and 18th century cottages. Shepherd's Green is on a dead end lane and this solitude enhances the period aura.

Greys Green stands alongside the main road but rows of cherry trees with large grass verges rich with daisies and buttercups have transformed it into a rather grand avenue. Cricket is still played on the green, opposite which stands the School Cottages, a row of pensioners' cottages dating from 1836.

Walk 14
ASTON
Length 2¾ miles

Ferry Lane, Aston.

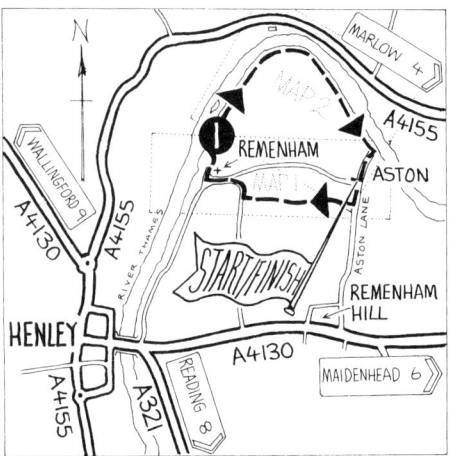

GETTING THERE: Aston is just off the A4130 between Henley and Maidenhead. From whichever direction you come enter Remenham Hill and take the turning to Aston (Aston Lane) and after a mile you enter the village. Either park around the Flower Pot Hotel or go down its right hand side and follow Ferry Lane where you can park by the slipway on the Thames.

MOORING: Upstream of Hambleden Lock (try the walk the other way round so that the Flower Pot is nearer the end).

TERRAIN: Mainly flat and no real problems with mud.

START: (GR 784842) From the Flower Pot Hotel head back up Aston Lane, past the old bridge abutments and then just past the last houses turn right by the 'Aston' sign, and go up the footpath.

INTRODUCTION: A popular, easy but ever rewarding stroll along the river with one of

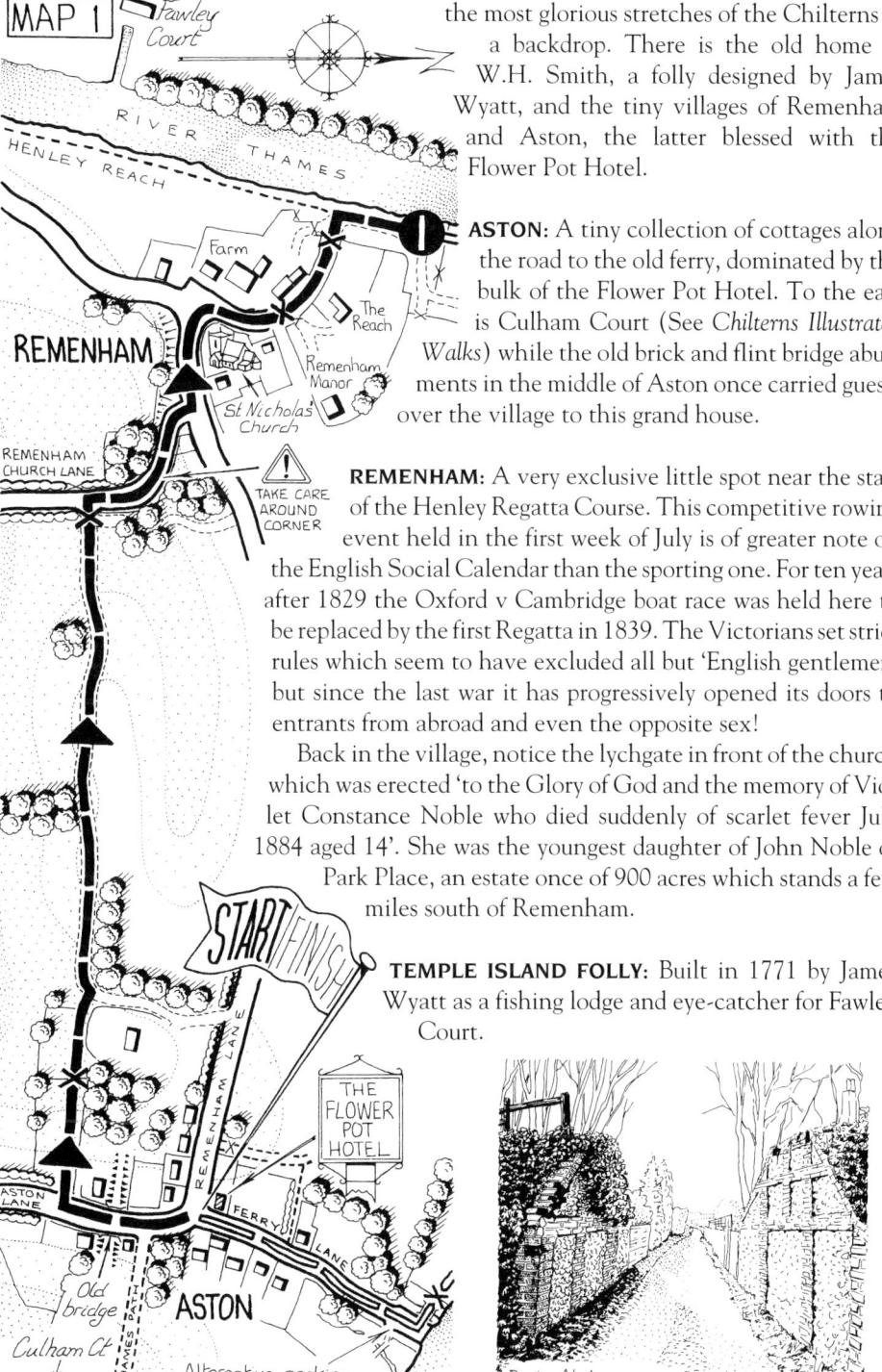

MAP 1

Fawley Court

RIVER THAMES

HENLEY REACH

Farm

The Reach

REMENHAM

Remenham Manor

St Nicholas Church

REMENHAM CHURCH LANE

⚠ TAKE CARE AROUND CORNER

START FINISH

THE FLOWER POT HOTEL

REMENHAM LANE

FERRY LANE

ASTON LANE

Old bridge

ASTON

Culham Ct

THAMES PATH

Alternative parking

the most glorious stretches of the Chilterns as a backdrop. There is the old home of W.H. Smith, a folly designed by James Wyatt, and the tiny villages of Remenham and Aston, the latter blessed with the Flower Pot Hotel.

ASTON: A tiny collection of cottages along the road to the old ferry, dominated by the bulk of the Flower Pot Hotel. To the east is Culham Court (See *Chilterns Illustrated Walks*) while the old brick and flint bridge abutments in the middle of Aston once carried guests over the village to this grand house.

REMENHAM: A very exclusive little spot near the start of the Henley Regatta Course. This competitive rowing event held in the first week of July is of greater note on the English Social Calendar than the sporting one. For ten years after 1829 the Oxford v Cambridge boat race was held here to be replaced by the first Regatta in 1839. The Victorians set strict rules which seem to have excluded all but 'English gentlemen' but since the last war it has progressively opened its doors to entrants from abroad and even the opposite sex!

Back in the village, notice the lychgate in front of the church which was erected 'to the Glory of God and the memory of Violet Constance Noble who died suddenly of scarlet fever July 1884 aged 14'. She was the youngest daughter of John Noble of Park Place, an estate once of 900 acres which stands a few miles south of Remenham.

TEMPLE ISLAND FOLLY: Built in 1771 by James Wyatt as a fishing lodge and eye-catcher for Fawley Court.

Bridge Abutments, Aston

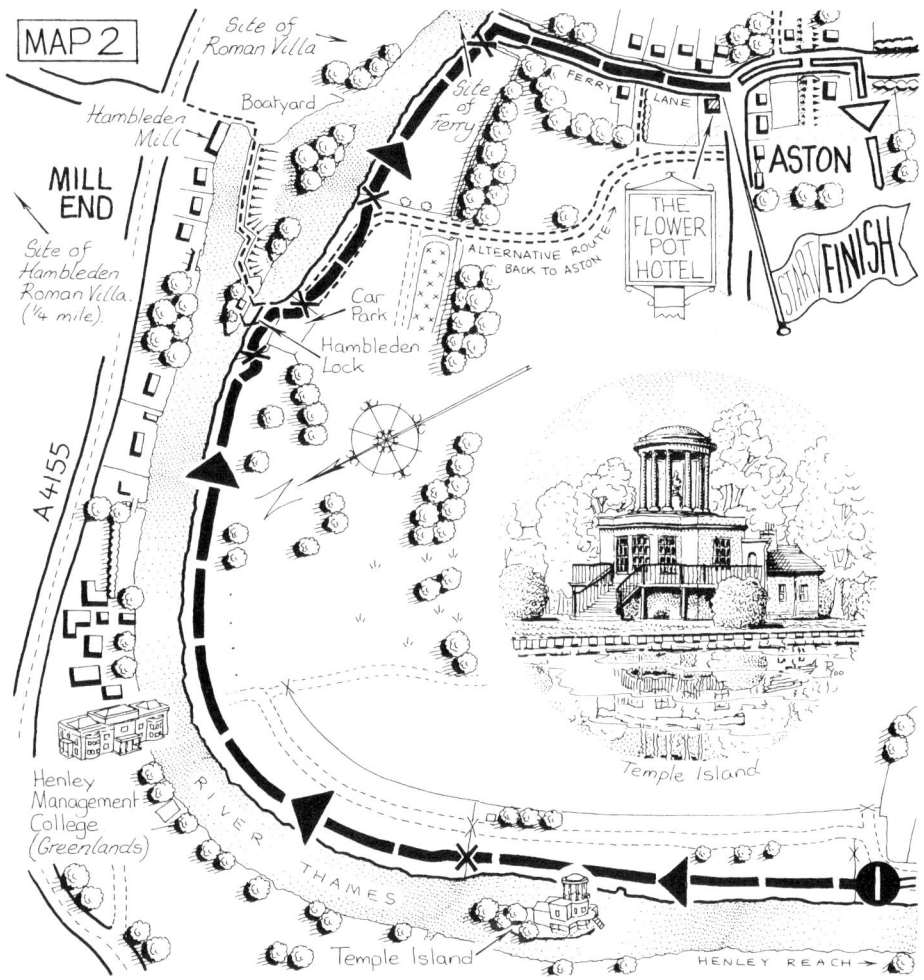

Temple Island

GREENLANDS (HENLEY MANAGEMENT COLLEGE): The original house here was destroyed in 1644 after a six month siege during the Civil War. It then became a farm until 1810 when the body of the present house was built, to then be further altered when it was owned by W.H. Smith, the newsagent, in the later 1800s.

MILL END: This Thames-side extension of the Hambleden parish is a collection of houses with a farm and mill on what was a busy site in Roman times. In 1911 a large villa was excavated revealing an extensive complex with grain storage and furnaces for drying. Aerial photography has revealed an additional villa site beside the river.

REFRESHMENTS:
THE FLOWER POT HOTEL. This large Victorian building with its exposed wood floor has the feel of a pub rather than a hotel. Good beer and home-made food with a well-positioned garden. Telephone: 01491 574721.

Walk 15
HURLEY
Length 5 miles

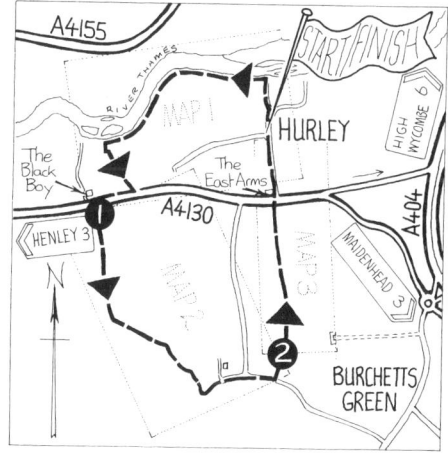

St Mary's Church + Hurley Priory

GETTING THERE: Hurley is just off the A4130 between Maidenhead and Henley. From whichever direction you approach turn down the road signposted 'Hurley Village Only', next to the East Arms. There is a car park at the end of the road near the church, but I have started the walk from the roadside spaces just past the Olde Bell.

MOORING: On the south side alongside the caravan park. Fee charged.

TERRAIN: One steady climb up to the Dewdrop Inn. The descent to Hurley is steep and can be slippery.

START: (GR 826837) With your back to the Olde Bell turn right and walk down the High Street, taking the left hand fork when

the road splits.

SHORT CUT: 2½ miles. Just before you reach the A4130 on Map 1, rather than cross the

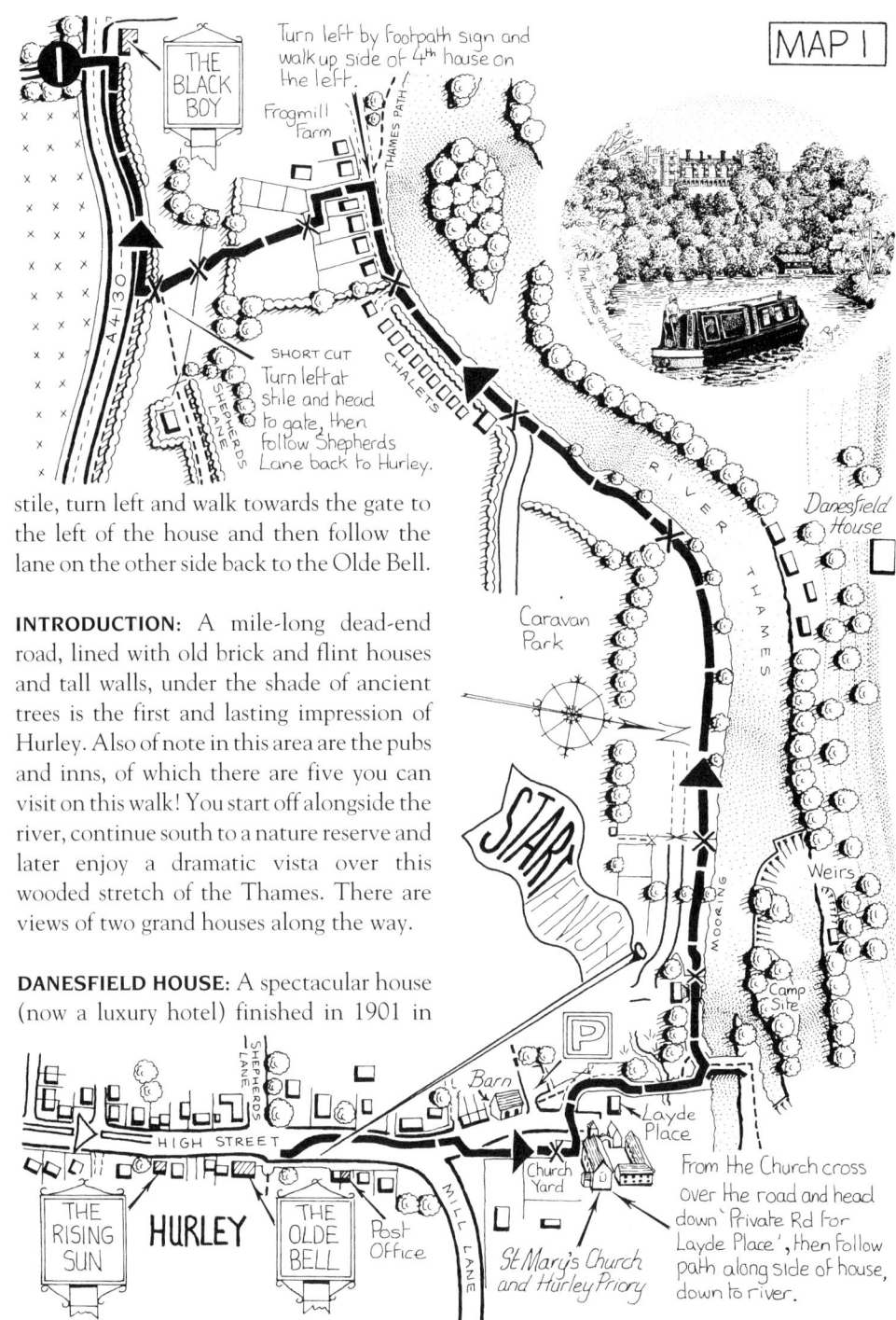

Turn left by footpath sign and walk up side of 4ᵗʰ house on the left.

THE BLACK BOY

Frogmill Farm

THAMES PATH

A 4130

SHORT CUT
Turn left at stile and head to gate, then follow Shepherds Lane back to Hurley.

SHEPHERDS LANE

CHALETS

MAP 1

RIVER THAMES

Danesfield House

Caravan Park

stile, turn left and walk towards the gate to the left of the house and then follow the lane on the other side back to the Olde Bell.

INTRODUCTION: A mile-long dead-end road, lined with old brick and flint houses and tall walls, under the shade of ancient trees is the first and lasting impression of Hurley. Also of note in this area are the pubs and inns, of which there are five you can visit on this walk! You start off alongside the river, continue south to a nature reserve and later enjoy a dramatic vista over this wooded stretch of the Thames. There are views of two grand houses along the way.

DANESFIELD HOUSE: A spectacular house (now a luxury hotel) finished in 1901 in

START FINISH

MOORING

Weirs

Camp Site

P

Barn

SHEPHERDS LANE

HIGH STREET

THE RISING SUN

HURLEY

THE OLDE BELL

Post Office

MILL LANE

Church Yard

St Mary's Church and Hurley Priory

Layde Place

From the Church cross over the road and head down 'Private Rd for Layde Place', then follow path along side of house, down to river.

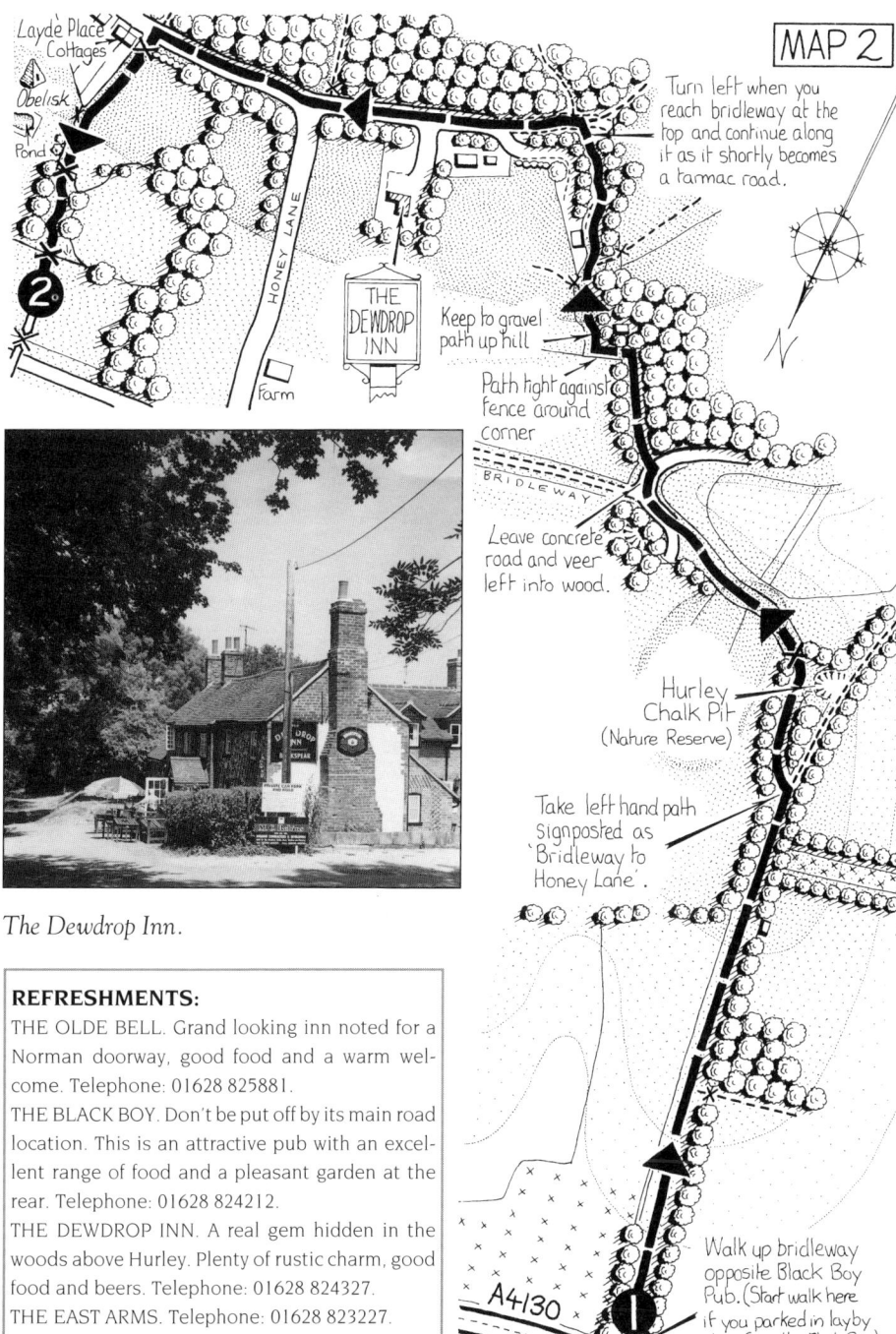

MAP 2

Layde Place Cottages

Obelisk

Pond

HONEY LANE

THE DEWDROP INN

Farm

Turn left when you reach bridleway at the top and continue along it as it shortly becomes a tarmac road.

Keep to gravel path up hill

Path tight against fence around corner

BRIDLEWAY

Leave concrete road and veer left into wood.

Hurley Chalk Pit (Nature Reserve)

Take left hand path signposted as 'Bridleway to Honey Lane'.

Walk up bridleway opposite Black Boy Pub. (Start walk here if you parked in layby along from the Black Boy).

A4130

The Dewdrop Inn.

REFRESHMENTS:

THE OLDE BELL. Grand looking inn noted for a Norman doorway, good food and a warm welcome. Telephone: 01628 825881.

THE BLACK BOY. Don't be put off by its main road location. This is an attractive pub with an excellent range of food and a pleasant garden at the rear. Telephone: 01628 824212.

THE DEWDROP INN. A real gem hidden in the woods above Hurley. Plenty of rustic charm, good food and beers. Telephone: 01628 824327.

THE EAST ARMS. Telephone: 01628 823227.

THE RISING SUN. Telephone: 01628 824274.

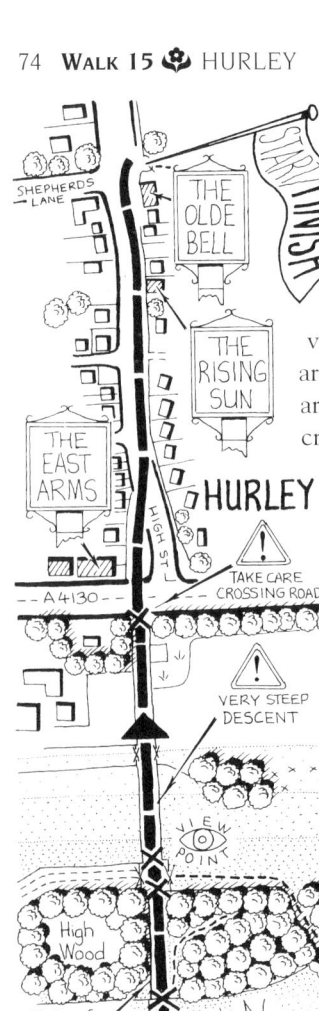

gleaming white chalk, an appropriate building material, as it was owned at that time by
the soap manufacturer Robert Hudson.

HURLEY CHALK PIT: This old chalk pit and the surrounding triangle of woodland form a nature reserve.
In springtime it is blessed with flowers like bluebells and
violets while as summer approaches look out for yellow
archangel, sanicle and white helleborine. Overhead the trees
are mainly beech, but there is oak, ash, field maple, wild cherry,
crab apple, whitebeam and silver birch. Above the pit itself
there is a small area of hazel coppice which is still cut once
every 10 years. Also of note are the twenty species of but-
terfly which have been spotted here.

HALL PLACE: This large red brick house was built in
the 1730s for William East (hence the East Arms pub
in Hurley). Also note the odd brick pyramidal obelisk
behind the Layde Place cottages.

HURLEY: Like neighbouring Bisham, Hurley grew
up around its priory. The remains of this Bene-
dictine establishment include St Mary's church
which is just the nave of the original priory church
and whose proportions indicate that it may be even
older than the Norman doors and windows would suggest. On its north side is a range of buildings which were
the priory refec-
tory while by the
road is a 14th
century barn and
in the garden of
the house oppo-
site the church is
a dovecote of the
same period. The
remainder of the
village is com-
posed of brick and flint houses, attractively aged
and set along the tree-lined road. A pleasant
break from all this brick is made by the fine
Arts and Crafts style semis dating from 1898
on your left as you return, a few houses down
from the East Arms.

Walk 16
COOKHAM DEAN
Length 3¼ miles

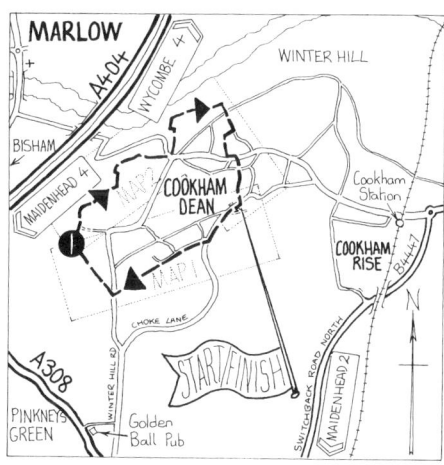

View of Marlow from Quarry Wood

GETTING THERE: Cookham Dean is situated between the A308 and the B4447 north of Maidenhead. Approaching from Maidenhead town centre take the A308 towards Marlow. As you leave the town the road makes a sharp left turn, then soon starts across the edge of Pinkneys Green where you take the first right turn (Winter Hill Road) towards Cookham Dean. After nearly a mile the road splits and you take the right hand fork (Choke Lane) and follow it as it bends left around the hill and into Cookham Dean. Parking is best opposite the Jolly Farmer pub, around the churchyard wall.

TERRAIN: An undulating walk with no large but a few sharp climbs. Can be muddy and a concrete path towards the end may be slippery – make sure your footwear is adequate!

START: (GR 871851) Facing the Jolly Farmer turn left and walk up Church Road (left hand side is best) until at the top of the hill you cross over and go down the road

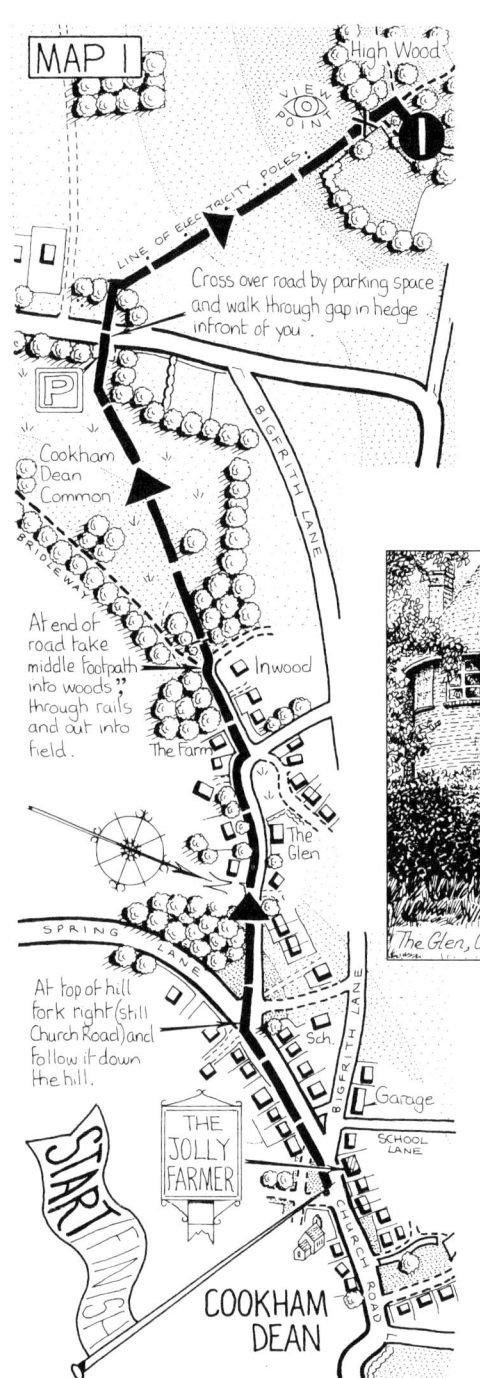

MAP I

High Wood

VIEW POINT

Cross over road by parking space and walk through gap in hedge in front of you.

LINE OF ELECTRICITY POLES

P

Cookham Dean Common

BIGFRITH LANE

BRIDLEWAY

At end of road take middle footpath into woods, through rails and out into field.

Inwood

The Farm

The Glen

SPRING LANE

At top of hill fork right (still Church Road) and follow it down the hill.

Sch

BIGFRITH LANE

START FINISH

THE JOLLY FARMER

Garage

SCHOOL LANE

CHURCH ROAD

COOKHAM DEAN

(still Church Road) which forks off to the right and follow it into the trees.

INTRODUCTION: A pleasantly surprising walk through strips of National Trust protected common land and one of the best woodland walks along the Thames. The highlight must be the excellent views over the river although the choice of three pubs on your return must run a close second.

COOKHAM DEAN: With its scattering of cottages set in steep but small dry valleys, Cookham Dean is more reminiscent of Welsh Border Country than the Home Counties!

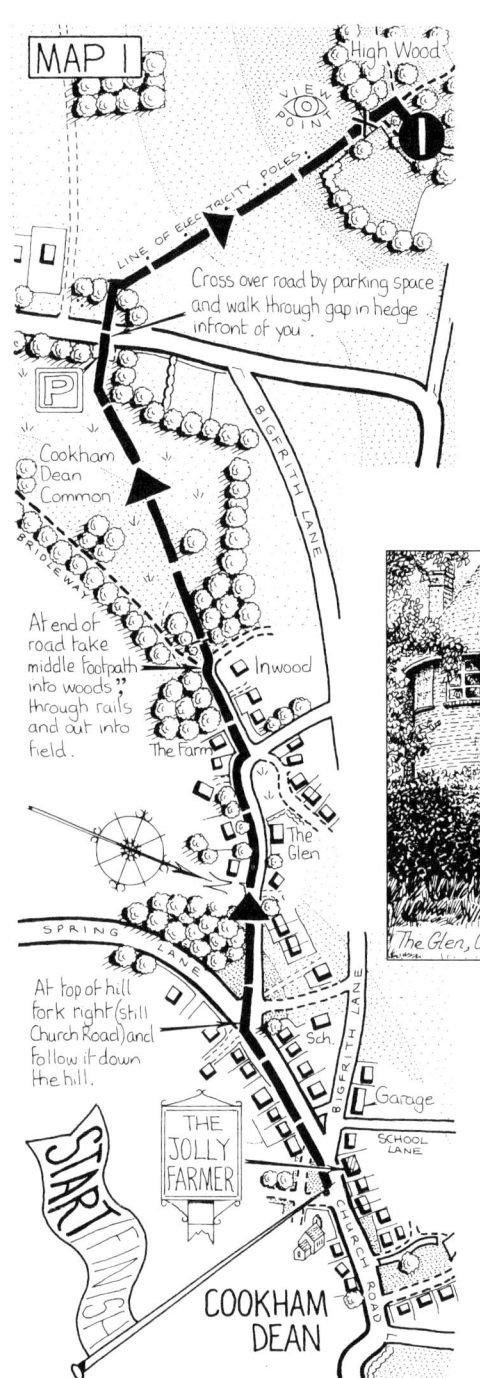

The Glen, Church Road.

Only a few hundred years ago the Dean was a disreputable place, the haunt of gypsies and poachers, who would escape the law by slipping into the next parish. The locals were little better, being called 'as rude as their surroundings and as lawless, almost, as their gypsy neighbours'. They were usually unrecorded labourers and their house plots were often illegally cut out of the woodland. Even the constable had a rough edge. He reported in 1812 that a certain Mol Smith had hit him in the face so he had retaliated by striking her twice!

This constable was also a fruiterer and

around this time the Dean became an important area for growing cherries. Orchards filled the valley and by 1900 nearly every house had its own cherry, apple and walnut trees. The local name for someone born in Cookham Dean is 'Kaffir'. This name probably comes partly from those returning from the Boer War but also from the Black Circassian cherries which in the local dialect were called 'cashers'.

Respectability reached the village with the building of the church in 1845 although it was founded as a missionary church, implying that there were still unconverted souls in these parts! The church may seem insignificant to us now but the design was so well received that it was copied a number of times including one in Tasmania.

The most notable resident in these parts was Kenneth Grahame who lived here as a boy and returned to a house called Mayfield (now Herries School) to write *The Wind in the Willows*.

STERLINGS: Another important resident was the fifth Earl of Sterling who built himself a house in the late 1600s (it stood on a site behind the church which had formerly been a grange for Bisham Abbey). The Sterlings had moved down into England with James I and their loyalty was rewarded with titles including 'Viscount of Canada' and with land including Long Island, New York! (It was known at the time as Island of Sterling.) Unfortunately the Sterlings became involved in failed colonisation schemes so they were driven out of their Canadian lands by the French and their rights to Long Island were not recognised. By the time the fifth Earl moved to Cookham Dean the family were broke and by the 1800s the house and their fortune had long since gone.

COOKHAM DEAN COMMON: The protection of strips of common land by the National Trust has helped retain an authentic open village layout in parts of Cookham Dean. Even more notable is the large field, just past Inwood, where any fan of grasses will be in heaven with the numerous different types on show.

QUARRY WOOD: Part of the strip of woodland which covers the steep escarpment, collectively known as Bisham Woods. It has one of the most diverse selection of trees in

SWEET CHESTNUT
Grows up to 30m high. Sharp toothed, long leaves. Deeply fissured bark. Introduced into this country especially for it's edible nuts.
up to 25cm

WYCH ELM
Grows up to 40m high. Leaves have one side curved around stalk. Clusters of papery fruit. Has been found to resist Dutch Elm Disease and is Britain's only common elm.
8-16cm

COMMON ASH
Grows up to 40m high. 7-13 leaflets per stalk. Distinctive black buds throughout winter. Huge clusters of winged fruits on female trees.
20-35cm

SYCAMORE
Grows up to 35m high. 5 toothed lobed leaves with red stalks. Pairs of winged fruits. Fast growing, invasive tree. Look out for numerous young trees.
10-15cm

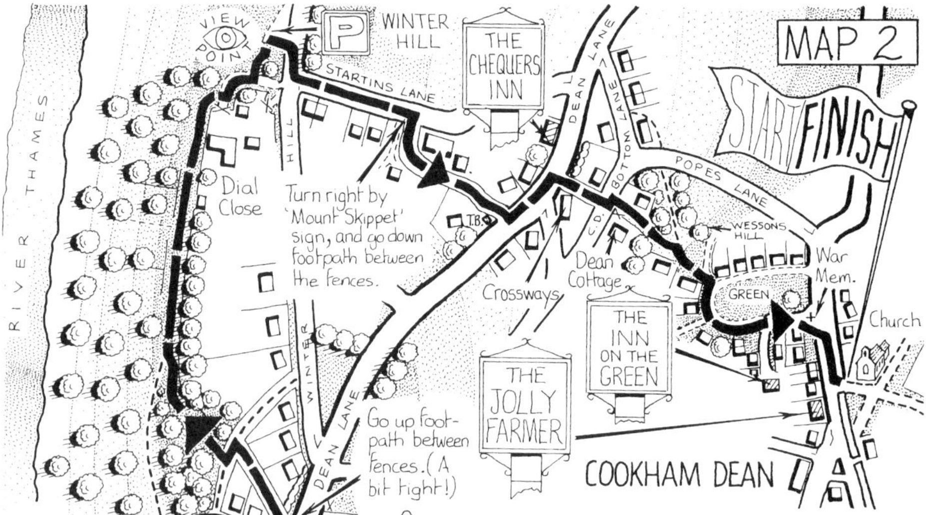

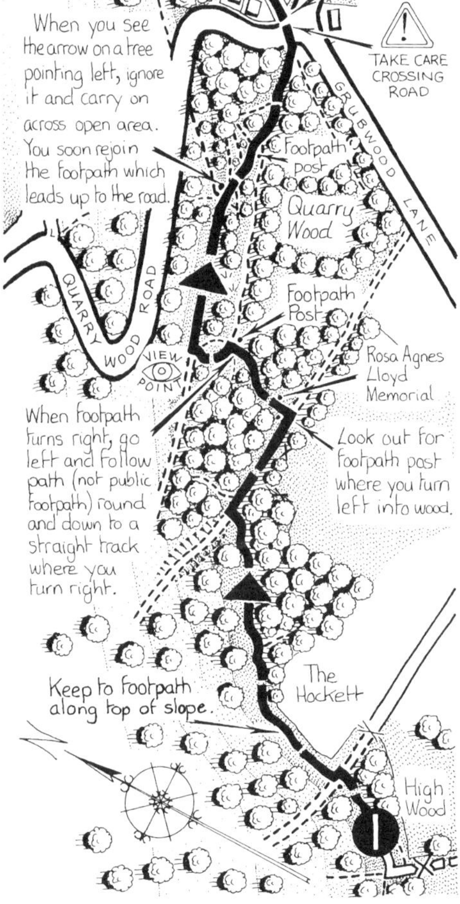

MAP 2

WINTER HILL

P

STARTINS LANE

THE CHEQUERS INN

DEAN LANE

BOTTOM LANE

POPES LANE

START FINISH

WESSONS HILL

GREEN

War Mem.

Church

Dial Close

Turn right by 'Mount Skippet' sign, and go down footpath between the fences.

T89

Crossways

Dean Cottage

THE INN ON THE GREEN

Go up footpath between fences. (A bit right!)

THE JOLLY FARMER

COOKHAM DEAN

WINTER HILL

DEAN LANE

When you see the arrow on a tree pointing left, ignore it and carry on across open area. You soon rejoin the footpath which leads up to the road.

TAKE CARE CROSSING ROAD

GRUBWOOD LANE

Footpath post

Quarry Wood

QUARRY WOOD ROAD

VIEW POINT

Footpath Post

Rosa Agnes Lloyd Memorial

When footpath turns right, go left and follow path (not public footpath) round and down to a straight track where you turn right.

Look out for footpath post where you turn left into wood.

Keep to footpath along top of slope.

The Hockett

High Wood

the county, and there are also spectacular views from the track above Quarry Wood Road. Somewhere in the woods is Lady Winifred's Seat, involved in the legend of the elopement of a monk from Bisham and a local lady. Her father followed them and when they refused to come down he fired his gun, but unfortunately shot his daughter! (The story is slightly flawed as the Abbey was abolished before guns became widely available.)

WINTER HILL: A well known local view point which probably gets its name from use as winter grazing when the land below was flooded.

REFRESHMENTS:

THE JOLLY FARMER. A quaint pub which was saved by a consortium of 34 local residents in the 1980s. Full of character with good food and garden with play area. Telephone: 01628 482905.

THE INN ON THE GREEN. Another rustic pub, noted for its food and smart restaurant. Telephone: 01628 482638.

THE CHEQUERS. Welcoming atmosphere with good food and well-kept ales. Telephone: 01628 481232.

HEDGERLEY

Length 4 miles

The White Horse, Hedgerley.

GETTING THERE: From junction 2 on the M40 take the A355 towards Slough and immediately turn left up the minor road by the timber yard. Follow this road alongside the motorway until the T junction where you turn right down Village Lane and on entering Hedgerley, park along the roadside by the White Horse. From Slough take the A355 towards Beaconsfield and after going through Farnham Common and past the garage turn right up One Pin Lane. Follow this over the crossroads by the pub of the same name and down into Hedgerley.

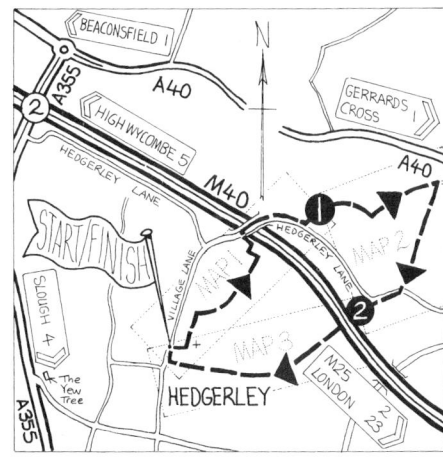

TERRAIN: One small climb from Hedgerley then afterwards mainly flat. Can be muddy along the bridleway at the start of the walk.

START: (GR 969874) With your back to the White Horse, turn left down Village Lane a few yards, then turn left up the path signposted to the church. Go up the short hill and then follow the bridleway as it takes a sharp left turn in front of the gate to the churchyard.

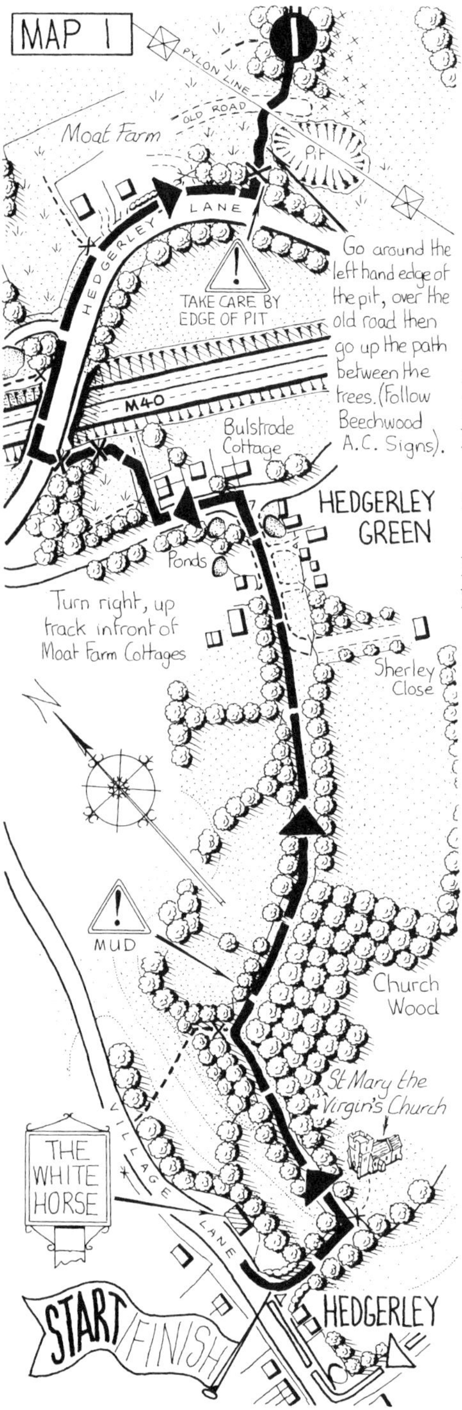

MAP 1

PYLON LINE

OLD ROAD

Moat Farm

LANE

HEDGERLEY LANE

P.H.

TAKE CARE BY EDGE OF PIT

Go around the left hand edge of the pit, over the old road then go up the path between the trees. (Follow Beechwood A.C. Signs).

M40

Bulstrode Cottage

HEDGERLEY GREEN

Ponds

Turn right, up track in front of Moat Farm Cottages

Sherley Close

MUD

Church Wood

St Mary the Virgin's Church

THE WHITE HORSE

VILLAGE LANE

START FINISH

HEDGERLEY

INTRODUCTION: One of the saving graces of the Chilterns is the tranquillity you can find remarkably close to towns and motorways, and Hedgerley is no exception. It has all the ingredients for the perfect village: brick and timber-framed cottages, a pond, a picturesque pub overlooked by the church, and the surrounding wooded hills and fields complete the recipe. In contrast the other end of this walk passes through the grand old Bulstrode Park, with oak-lined avenues and sweeping grass slopes, while in between is the isolated Hedgerley Green, and Church Wood Nature Reserve.

HEDGERLEY: Unlike most Chiltern villages there is evidence of early settlement in the Hedgerley area. Most notable are two Roman kilns, one found at Fulmer and the other just west of Moat Farm. There is also believed to have been a Roman road running in part from just south of the Iron Age hillfort across Bulstrode Park and then roughly along the line of the M40 from Moat Farm.

St Mary the Virgin Church.

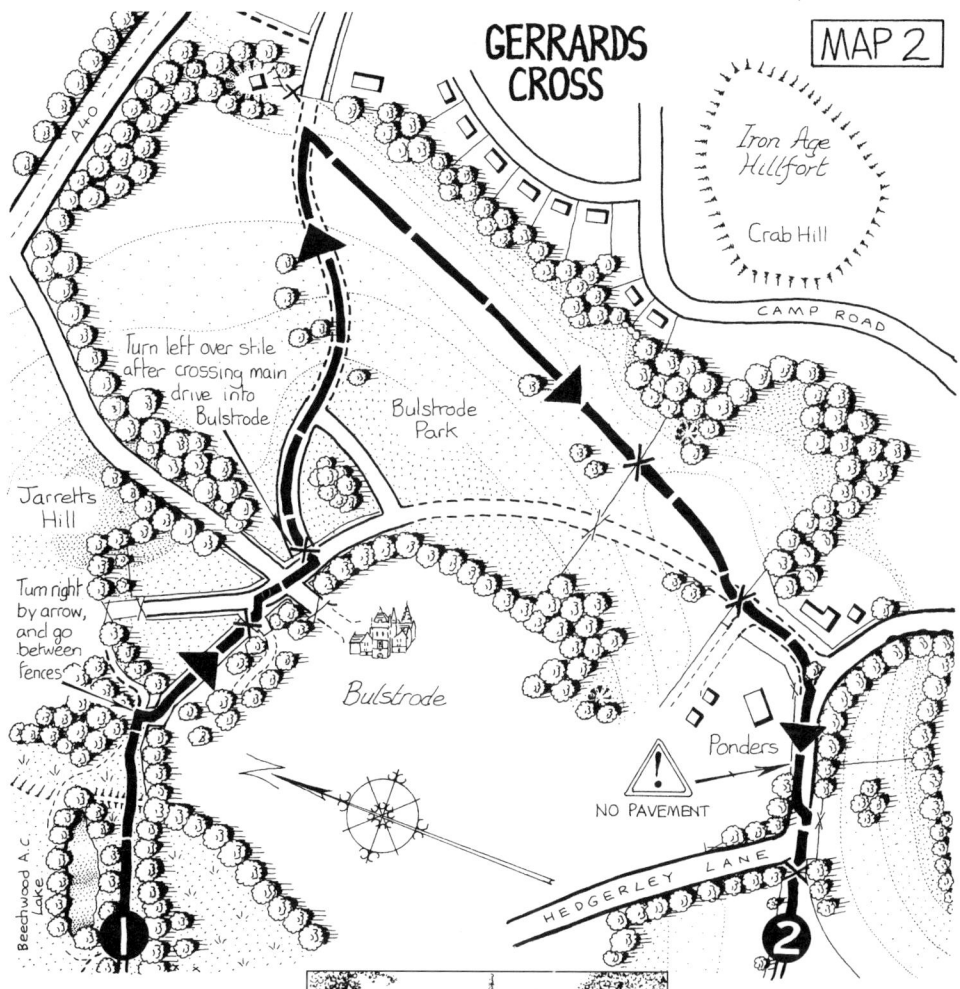

GERRARDS CROSS

MAP 2

Iron Age Hillfort

Crab Hill

CAMP ROAD

Turn left over stile after crossing main drive into Bulstrode

Bulstrode Park

Jarretts Hill

Turn right by arrow, and go between fences

Bulstrode

Beechwood A.C. Lake

NO PAVEMENT

Ponders

HEDGERLEY LANE

Bulstrode

The village itself comprises a line of cottages, a good number having earlier 17th century timber frames with a later brick front added as was the fashion (the White Horse and Dean Cottages are examples). Dramatically set on a prominence above the pub stands St Mary the Virgin's church, built in 1852, and containing a framed shred of fabric which is said to be all that remains of a gift from Charles II. The story goes that the 17th century King (though it could have been his father) visited the village and when he saw the poor state of the altar cloth, he draped his own cloak over it as a replacement! Also of note are the pulpit and some pieces of furniture which were carved from satinwood, rescued from a

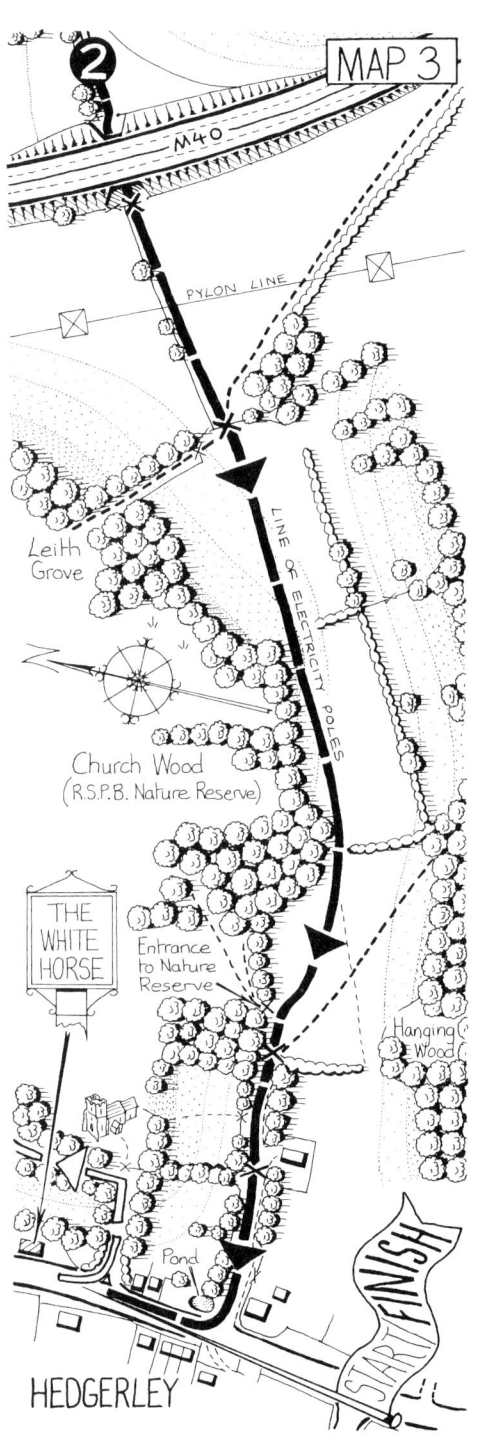

church in Antigua which was demolished by an earthquake in 1853!

HEDGERLEY GREEN: An attractively set collection of renovated cottages approached along a rectilinear green and surrounding a number of tree-lined ponds. A real isolated gem!

MOAT FARM: Part of the moat from which the farm is named survives, and the discovery of flint foundations and medieval pottery backs up the theory that it was a 13th century site belonging to the Knights Templars.

BULSTRODE PARK: The current red brick mansion – which you can only get a glimpse of through the entrance – was built in the 1860s. It replaced an earlier house built for the notorious Judge Jeffreys in the 1680s and which had been remodelled in 1806-9 for the Duke of Portland, the then Prime Minister. The sweeping open grounds you walk through still retain some of the atmosphere of the original 18th century design.

Part of the park on Crab Hill was sold off, and from 1930 an exclusive housing estate formed here around the remains of the largest Iron Age hillfort in Buckinghamshire. The double ramparts enclosed an area which had been excavated earlier but any finds indicated only a short term occupation.

HOLYPORT

Length 3 miles

Holyport Green

GETTING THERE: Holyport lies between the A330 and the A308 west of Windsor. Approaching from Maidenhead town centre take the A308 towards Windsor and at the A308(M) roundabout take the A330 to Holyport. Go over the motorway and along the red brick wall on your left, until you enter The Green where you take your first left. Parking is best alongside the roads off to the left; please stop by the fences and not in front of the houses.

TERRAIN: All flat but can be damp under foot.

START: (GR 892778) From The Green walk down Holyport Street (which runs from behind the war memorial shelter by the pond) and past the Belgian Arms.

INTRODUCTION: The neat and trim green together with a ring of grand houses and rustic cottages and a duckpond surrounded by willows make Holyport an idyllic village.

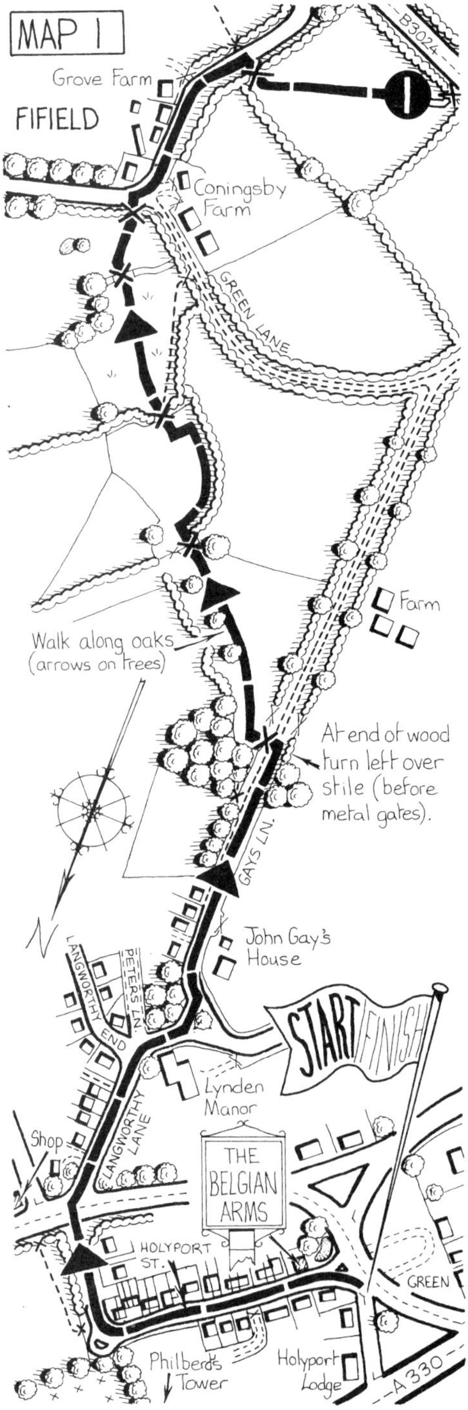

MAP 1

Grove Farm

FIFIELD

Coningsby Farm

GREEN LANE

B3024

Walk along oaks (arrows on trees)

At end of wood turn left over stile (before metal gates).

Farm

GAYS LN.

John Gay's House

N

LANGWORTHY END

PETERS LN.

START FINISH

Lynden Manor

Shop

LANGWORTHY LANE

THE BELGIAN ARMS

HOLYPORT ST.

GREEN

Philberd's Tower

Holyport Lodge

A330

The walk from here takes you along back lanes and across fields of grass littered with ponds and streams. You pass Philberd's Tower, old manor houses and farms to return to Holyport which is a pub-rich zone with a choice of four to visit!

HOLYPORT: Holyport as a name is misleading. The 'port' element has no connection with water and actually means 'a market' while the 'Holy' part derives from the Saxon word 'hori' meaning 'muddy'! An Anglo-Saxon settlement was discovered under a layer of peat to the north of the current village. Brushwood floors and wooden uprights were uncovered and these building remains were dated to the 8th century. There is also a known Saxon road passing to the south.

If there was a market it was probably in the area of the green, and Holyport Street would have run between it and the manor house. This road is lined with notable timber-framed houses, some dating back as far as the 14th century (Hamble Cottage), and its current dead-end status has preserved this peaceful strip of history. From the end of the street you can see Philberd's Tower. This brick oddity (which I assume is

Philberd's Tower

Holyport Street.

a water tower) stands on the site of the last Philberd's Manor which was demolished early last century. It was the third such house on the site, although all that remains of the original medieval house of the Philibert family is the old moat.

The second manor house was the home of Nell Gwyn, the notorious mistress of Charles II. The King would dine with his friend the Duke of Buckingham in Windsor and then they would ride cross country to visit Nell at Holyport. She gave birth to his son in 1670 and after making an outburst at Court, Charles made him the Earl of Burford. Nell died in 1687 and was buried at St Martin in the Fields, London.

Another historic site here is Holyport Grange (off Holyport Street) where in 1890 a famous court was opened for Real Tennis. More notable, although mundane, was the patented construction method for the walls and floor, a system which is still used for racquet sports today!

REFRESHMENTS:

THE BELGIAN ARMS. Previously called the Eagle, but renamed when prisoners of war saluted the pub while passing by. Picturesque setting behind the duckpond. Telephone: 01628 634468.

THE GEORGE. Originally a 16th century cottage which still retains character with its prominent position on The Green. Next door is an old brick brewhouse dating from the 18th century. Telephone: 01628 628317.

THE SUN AND STARS. On the B3024 south-west of Fifield. Closed on Sunday evening. Telephone: 01628 623639.

THE WHITE HART. Moneyrow Green, towards the B3024. Telephone: 01628 621460.

FIFIELD: Although the main part of the present village lies further east than this walk, the oldest part of the settlement was probably along Coningsby Lane, where there is an attractive set of timber-framed and brick private houses. The most notable visitor to this area must be King Haakon of Norway who lived at the nearby Folijohn

Park during the Nazi occupation of his country in the Second World War. After leaving Coningsby Lane you join the B3024 which runs along the line of the Saxon road between Reading and Windsor.

Grove Farm, Fifield.

STUD GREEN: Just over the A330 bridge is a right turn leading to Stud Green. The name is first mentioned in 1761 and probably relates to horses (previous to this it was known as Stert Green). At the far end is Stud Green Farmhouse dating from 1600, while on the right are lakes which are the remains of clay pits used in the local 19th century brickmaking industry.

The Old Brewhouse, The George.

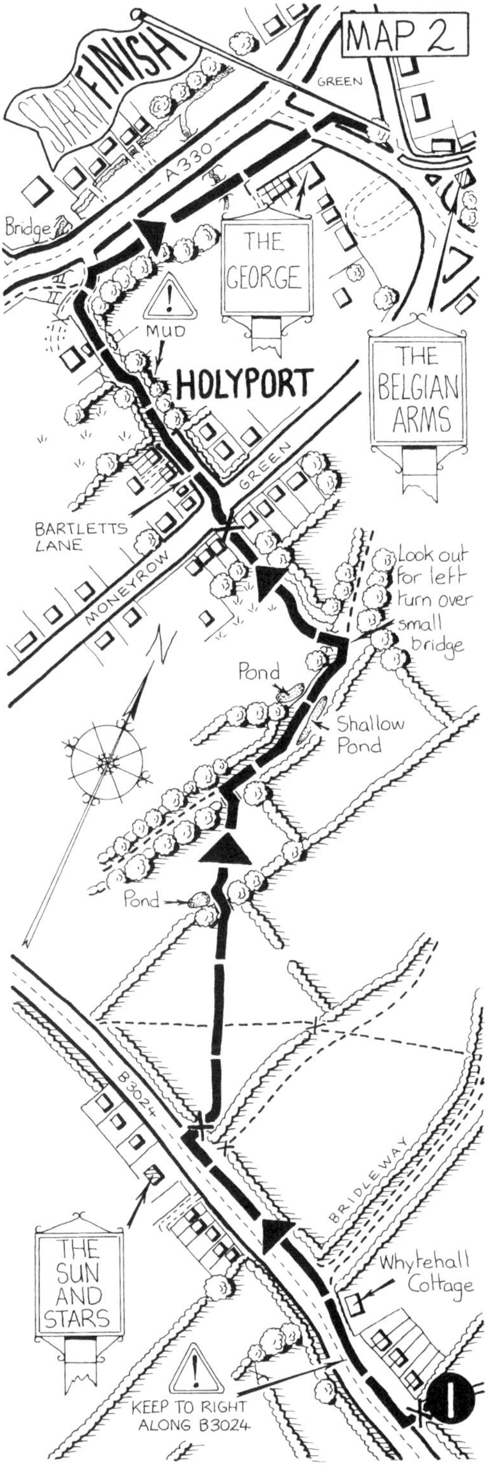

Walk 19
ETON
Length 5 miles

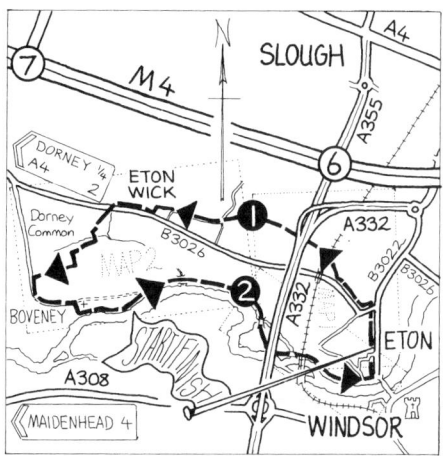

Eton College Chapel

GETTING THERE: Eton has to be approached from the north. From Maidenhead take the A4 towards Slough, turn right at the Sainsbury's roundabout down the B3026, through Dorney, and follow it into Eton. From Slough town centre take the A332 south, under the motorway and then at the roundabout take the B3022 to Eton.

To park in Eton for the duration of a walk your need to use one of the pay and display car parks. An alternative is to park along Eton Wick Road as you enter the town from Maidenhead, on the left by the red brick college buildings (avoid blocking accesses).

MOORING: Along the Brocas, upstream of Windsor Bridge.

TERRAIN: All flat and only one stile!

START: (GR 966774) Assuming you have parked in the town centre then the walk starts from outside the Henry VI pub, where the road to the car parks meets the High

Street. (The alternative start along Eton Wick Road is at GR 964779.)

INTRODUCTION: Although on a map it seems trapped between motorways, air routes and tourist attractions, this walk is remarkably peaceful, passing through an ancient landscape, a thousand years away from the surrounding modernity. Meadows and open commons with cattle grazing, a Thames-side stroll with views of Windsor Castle, the magnificent architecture of Eton College – all are features of the route, while

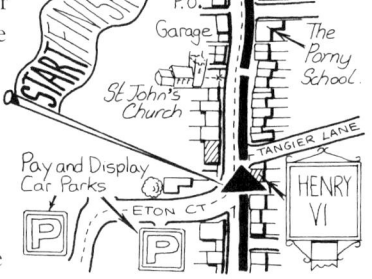

a choice of seven pubs awaits you in the town.

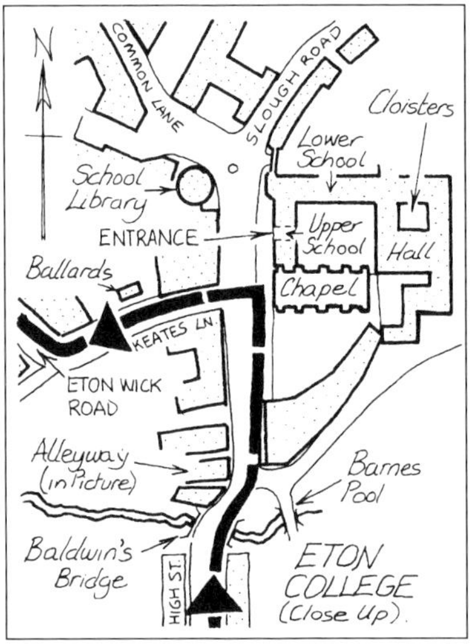

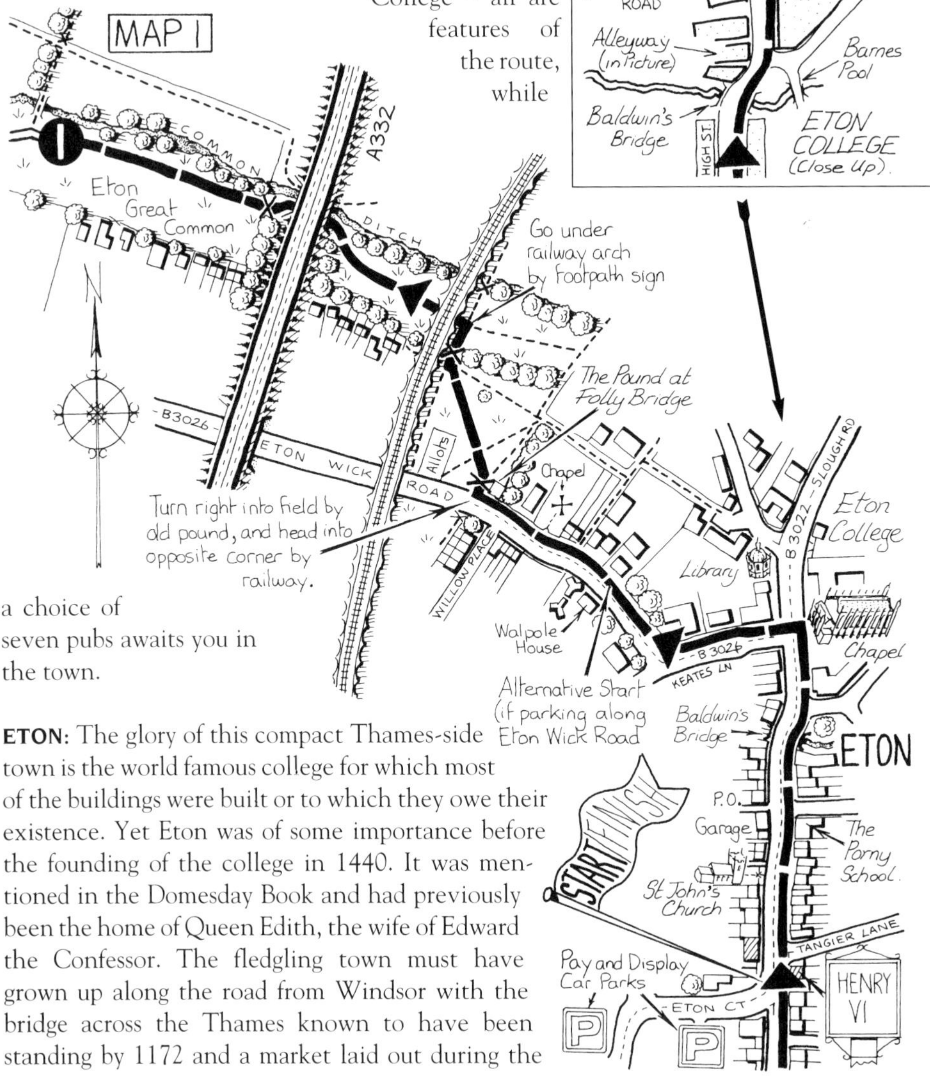

ETON: The glory of this compact Thames-side town is the world famous college for which most of the buildings were built or to which they owe their existence. Yet Eton was of some importance before the founding of the college in 1440. It was mentioned in the Domesday Book and had previously been the home of Queen Edith, the wife of Edward the Confessor. The fledgling town must have grown up along the road from Windsor with the bridge across the Thames known to have been standing by 1172 and a market laid out during the following century in the area below Baldwin's Bridge.

All signs of this early settlement have been swept aside by later building except for the surrounding lands which unlike the vast majority of the country were never enclosed. This in layman's terms means that the open common lands to the west of the town still exist and are one of the most characteristic features of this walk.

ETON COLLEGE: Virtually all the buildings to the north of Baldwin's Bridge are the schools and boarding houses which make up 'The King's College of Our Lady of Eton beside Windsor', or Eton College to you and me! It was founded in 1440 by King Henry VI who at the time was only 18 years old. Unlike his father Henry V, who demonstrated his ruthlessness in his victory at Agincourt, the younger Henry was a true Christian and pacifist, attributes which were inappropriate in the violent 15th century. Despite this, the King allowed his love of architecture to manifest itself in two great foundations. Inspired by William of Wykeham who had founded Winchester as a counterpart to his own New College, Oxford, Henry founded Eton and then its counterpart, King's College, Cambridge, the following year (the intake of students at King's College, Cambridge came exclusively from Eton right up to 1870).

The earliest and still most significant building at Eton was the College Chapel. The King had gained rights to the parish church at Eton in 1438 and started building the chapel just to the north of it in 1441 (the parish church was demolished in around 1480). Yet this is not the building you see today, for after eight years what had been constructed was pulled down, it is said in order to execute a more ambitious plan, although there is the possibility it was a bit

of a 'cowboy job'! We know of this rebuilding firstly because the inside face of a lot of the existing stonework has been carved, meaning it was originally facing outside and was re-used, and secondly the stone came from Caen in France which England lost control of in 1449 and hence would have been unable to ship any stone over for the revised chapel. The current building is only half the size of the proposed second design, with the small ante-chapel being built at right angles across the west end in place of what would have been a huge nave.

The 20th century also left its mark on the chapel, with new stained glass due to damage from an air raid in 1940 and most surprisingly a new ceiling! The famous fan vault which crowns this Perpendicular masterpiece is actually stone-faced concrete suspended on a steel frame which was built in the 1950s.

To the north are the Cloisters, Hall and Lower School which were built around the same time as the chapel, unusually for this area from brick, made just up the road at Slough. It was not until 1694 that the Upper School range was built to finally enclose the quadrangle. Across the road from here is the

Alleyway, Eton.

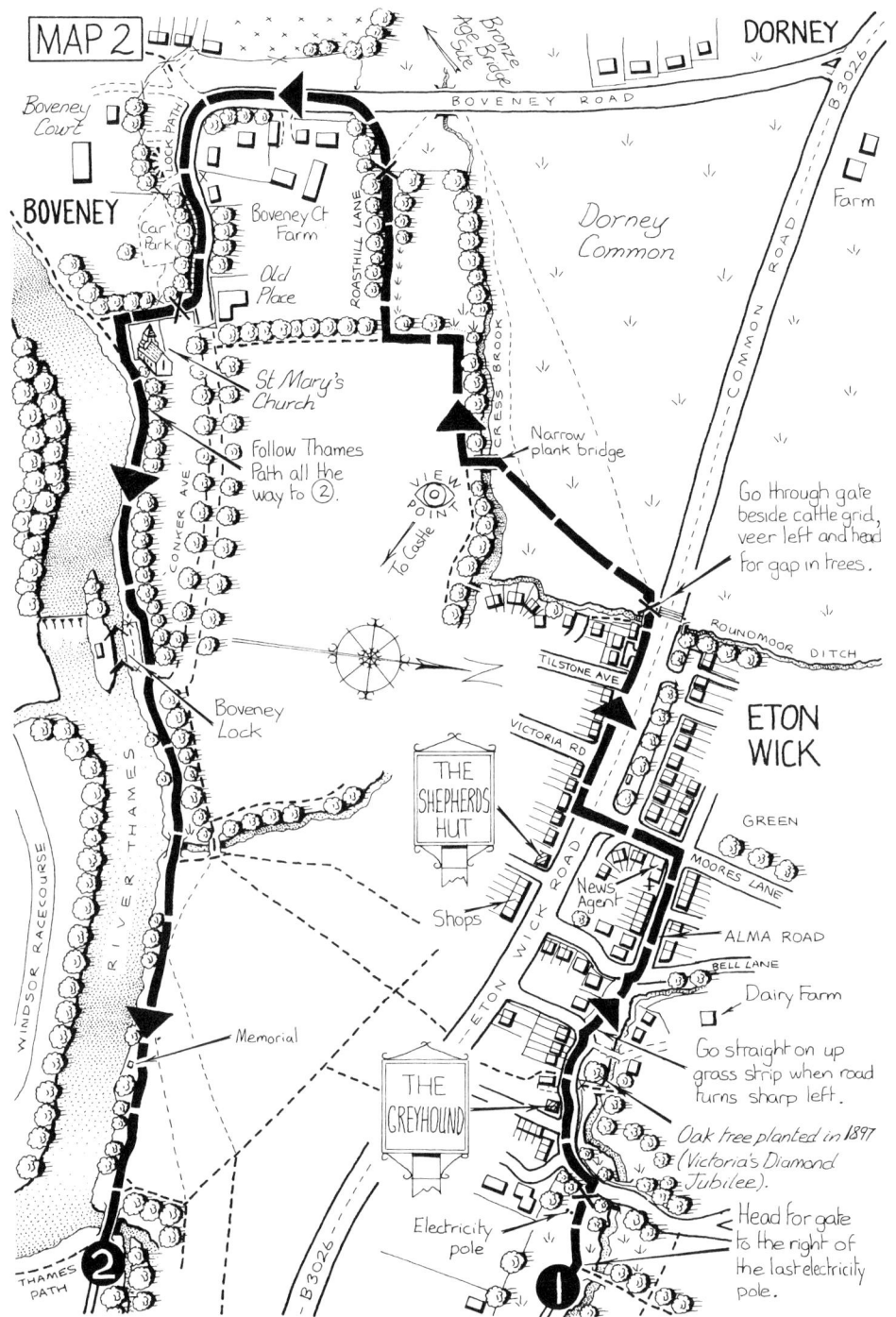

MAP 2

DORNEY

BOVENEY ROAD

Boveney Court

BOVENEY

Car Park

Boveney Ct Farm

ROASTHILL LANE

Old Place

Bronze Age Bridge Site

Dorney Common

CRESS BROOK

Farm

COMMON ROAD

B 3026

St Mary's Church

Follow Thames Path all the way to ②.

CONKER AVE

VIEW POINT

To Castle

Narrow plank bridge

Go through gate beside cattle grid, veer left and head for gap in trees.

ROUNDMOOR DITCH

Boveney Lock

TILSTONE AVE

ETON WICK

N

VICTORIA RD

THE SHEPHERDS HUT

GREEN

MOORES LANE

News Agent

ALMA ROAD

WINDSOR RACECOURSE

RIVER THAMES

ETON WICK ROAD

Shops

BELL LANE

Dairy Farm

Go straight on up grass strip when road turns sharp left.

Oak tree planted in 1897 (Victoria's Diamond Jubilee).

Memorial

THE GREYHOUND

Electricity pole

Head for gate to the right of the last electricity pole.

B 3026

THAMES PATH

②

①

South Door, St Marys, Boveney.

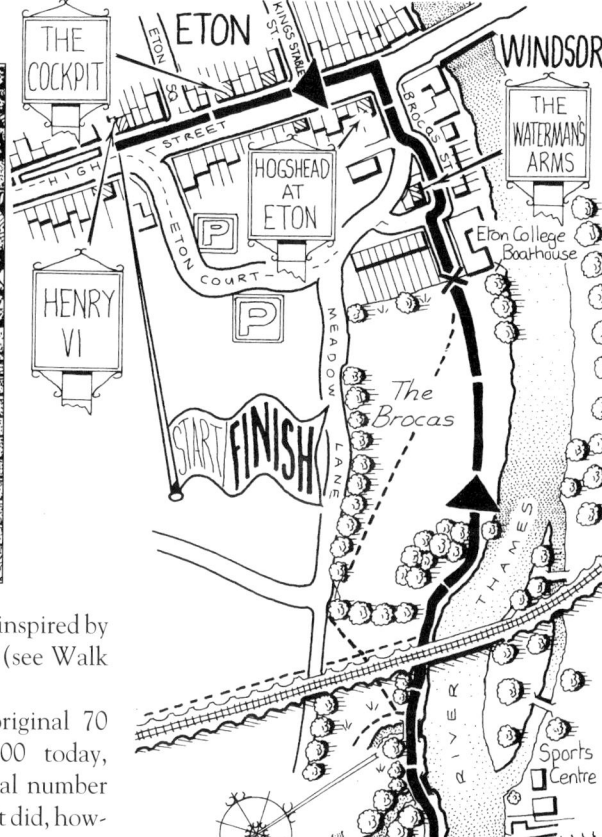

domed school library, which was inspired by the Radcliffe Camera in Oxford (see Walk 1) but was only built in 1908.

The college grew from its original 70 scholars to approximately 1,100 today, though there are still the original number who pay only reduced or no fees. It did, however, gain a reputation for fighting amongst the pupils (the son of the Earl of Shaftsbury was killed in a fracas in 1825) and for equal violence from the staff. The most notorious master was John Keate who could give the birch to up to 80 students in one day. Once on finding a group of boys standing outside his room he immediately flogged the lot of them before realising they were his divinity class waiting for their lesson!

Eton College and Chapel are open to the public at selected times.

ETON WICK: Essentially a 19th and 20th century creation, but there are ancient fragments like Bell Farmhouse, on Bell Lane, which was standing before Eton College was even thought of!

REFRESHMENTS:

I have recorded six pubs along the route through Eton, so there should be something for everyone here.

BOVENEY: A small hamlet comprising a few private houses and an isolated church. St Mary's position by the Thames is probably due to an ancient wharf which once stood here for loading timber from Windsor Forest. Old pictures of the church show it surrounded by gravestones though these have mysteriously disappeared! Near the church is Old Place, once a row of cottages which were converted into a charming single house in 1905, while hidden from view to the west is Boveney Court dating from the 15th century.

BRONZE AGE BRIDGE: Despite the world-wide fame of Henley Regatta, the Thames does not make a world class rowing course. Hence Eton College started to build in the 1990s a new rowing lake on the land to the west of Boveney. One advantage of this was that archaeologists were allowed to excavate the site prior to digging the course.

They found a Roman farmstead, Bronze Age barrows and enclosures, and earlier signs of activity dating back 8,000 years! But most important were the lines of vertical timbers unearthed in what is now a disused channel but was in prehistory the main course of the Thames. These turned out to be supports for a bridge constructed over 3,000 years ago, making it the earliest known across the Thames!

THE BROCAS: Named after the Brocas family from France who once owned the land, before it was later given to Eton College by Henry Bost while he was Provost from 1477 to 1504.

Windsor Castle

Walk 20
ENGLEFIELD GREEN
Length 3 miles

![Air Forces Memorial illustration]

Air Forces Memorial.

GETTING THERE: Englefield Green lies on the A328 which runs between the A30 and the A308 at Runnymede. Approaching from Windsor take the A308 towards Staines. Go through Old Windsor and then turn right up the A328 to Englefield Green. Just past the top of the hill at the round-about take the right hand fork and then your first right turn and park along the edge of the green near the Barley Mow pub.

MOORING: Along the bank at Runnymede (National Trust charge).

TERRAIN: Runnymede is often flooded, so I suggest this is a walk for summer or at least take good boots! The track down Cooper's Hill can also be very muddy. There is one steady climb.

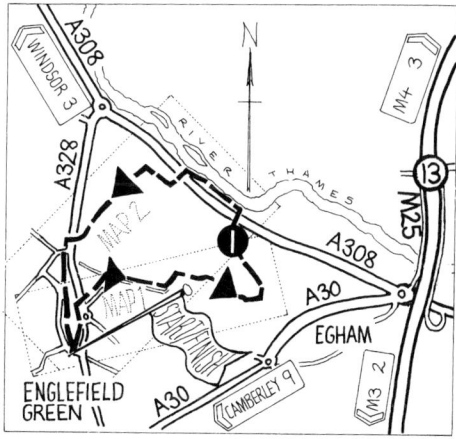

START: (GR 991714) With your back to the Barley Mow walk across the green towards the roundabout.

INTRODUCTION: Despite being a mere 3

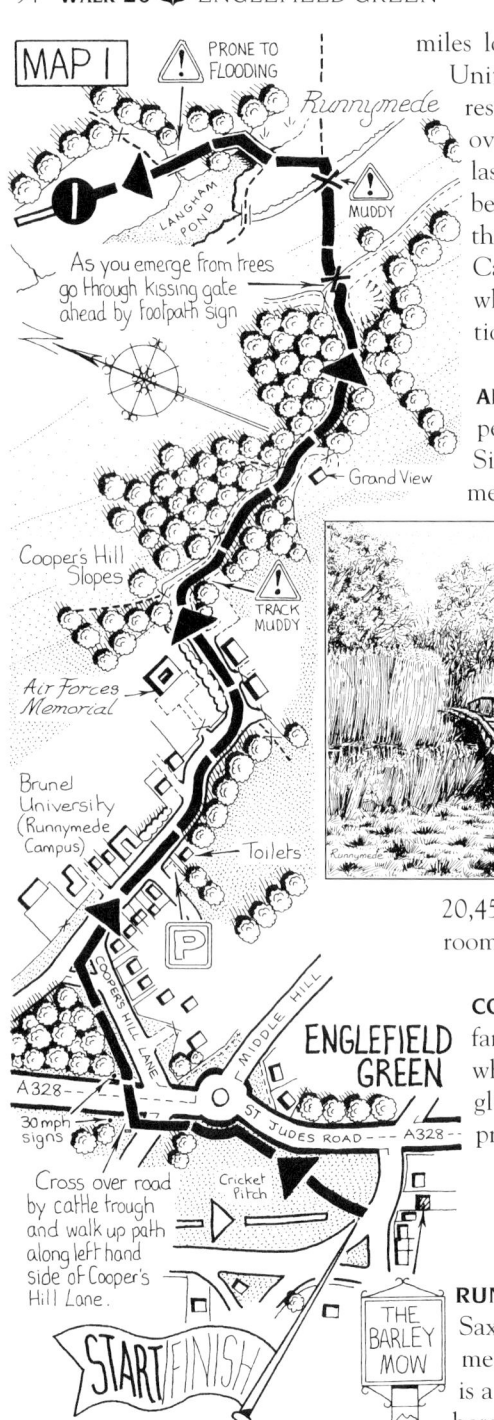

MAP 1

PRONE TO FLOODING

Runnymede

MUDDY

LANGHAM POND

As you emerge from trees go through kissing gate ahead by footpath sign

Grand View

Cooper's Hill Slopes

TRACK MUDDY

Air Forces Memorial

Brunel University (Runnymede Campus)

Toilets

P

COOPER'S HILL LANE

MIDDLE HILL

ENGLEFIELD GREEN

A328

30 mph signs

ST JUDES ROAD --- A328 --

Cross over road by cattle trough and walk up path along left hand side of Cooper's Hill Lane.

Cricket Pitch

THE BARLEY MOW

START / FINISH

miles long this walk passes through part of the United States of America! You also visit the resting place for thousands of airmen from all over the Commonwealth and the site of the last fatal duel held in England although it was between two Frenchmen. The international theme is completed by a visit to the Magna Carta monument, celebrating the document which influenced the American Constitution.

AIR FORCES MEMORIAL: This dramatically peaceful edifice (open daily) was designed by Sir Edward Maufe to commemorate the airmen killed in World War II who have no known grave. Around 25,000 relatives were present along with the Queen at the opening ceremony in 1953. Within the quadrangle are tablets like pages of a book, recording some 20,455 names, while above is an observation room, not dissimilar to a control tower.

COOPER'S HILL: These tree-clad slopes are a famous beauty spot although the woods limit what should be splendid views to occasional glimpses. Sir John Denham clearly had no problems in the 17th century when he wrote:
'My eye descending from this hill, surveys,
Where Thames among the wanton
valleys strays...'

RUNNYMEDE: The name implies it was a Saxon meeting place (from Old English 'rune' meaning council or speech and 'moed' which is a meadow). There was probably no building here as the Saxons often used open spaces for

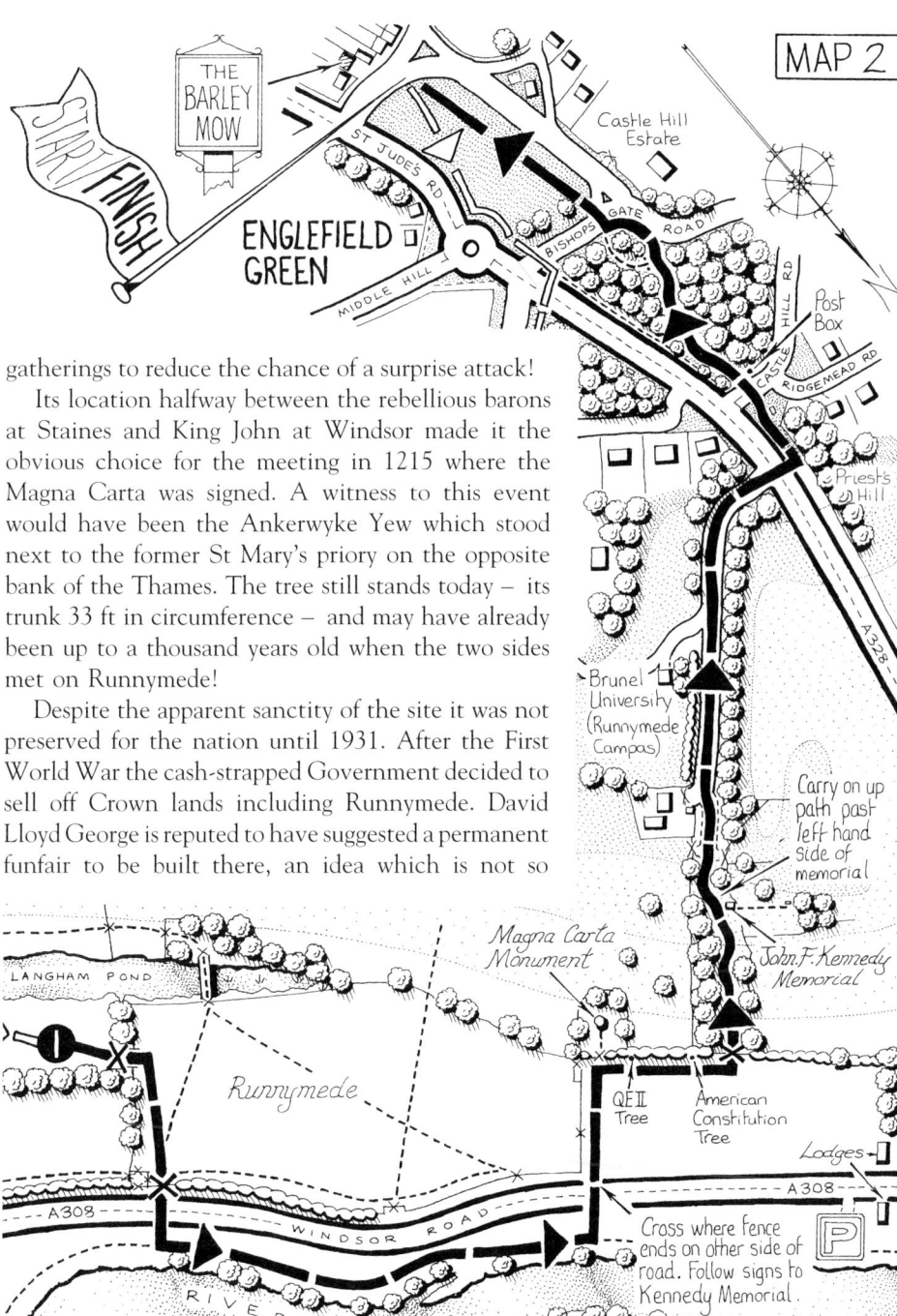

gatherings to reduce the chance of a surprise attack!

Its location halfway between the rebellious barons at Staines and King John at Windsor made it the obvious choice for the meeting in 1215 where the Magna Carta was signed. A witness to this event would have been the Ankerwyke Yew which stood next to the former St Mary's priory on the opposite bank of the Thames. The tree still stands today – its trunk 33 ft in circumference – and may have already been up to a thousand years old when the two sides met on Runnymede!

Despite the apparent sanctity of the site it was not preserved for the nation until 1931. After the First World War the cash-strapped Government decided to sell off Crown lands including Runnymede. David Lloyd George is reputed to have suggested a permanent funfair to be built there, an idea which is not so ludicrous as it might seem as there was a popular racecourse here in the 18th and 19th centuries (it only ceased to be used when the police refused to supply officers for a meeting in 1886). The site was eventually purchased by Lady Fairhaven and she had the famous architect Lutyens build the two lodges beside Windsor Road. Objectors who saw this as an infringement of common rights sprayed the buildings with creosote, which no amount of shuffling of foliage could disguise the next day when they were opened by the Prince of Wales!

Today the wetland nature of Runnymede makes the ornithologist or botanist as much at home as the historian.

MAGNA CARTA MONUMENT: Two boards as you walk up to the rotunda give a detailed account of the events of 1215 so I will not dwell on them here. The monument itself was paid for by the American Bar Association and built with a single pillar of English granite under a rotunda, the top of which resembles a flying saucer out of a 1950s' B-movie! In the hedge between here and the

Kennedy Memorial are two trees, one planted by the Queen, the other in soil from Jamestown, USA, to commemorate the bicentenary of the American Constitution.

THE KENNEDY MEMORIAL: In 1964 the Prime Minister announced that 'an acre of Runnymede' should be given 'in perpetuity to the United States in memory of President Kennedy'. Unfortunately they had not consulted the National Trust who under the agreement made when they were given the land by Lady Fairhaven in 1931 were not allowed to transfer it to another owner. This is why the memorial stands in three acres of land which was hastily found adjoining Runnymede and not the one acre stated on the stone itself. There was further insult in 1968 when it was damaged by a bomb (you can just make out fine cracks on the surface) and then in 1974 when it was toppled and daubed in paint! A notice board at the start of the path explains the themes behind the memorial and rightly warns that the granite steps, which represent the Pilgrim's Progress, can be slippery!

ENGLEFIELD GREEN: On Priest's Hill just beyond the green in 1845 two exiled Frenchmen took positions for a duel. One of the men called Cournet was wounded in the fight and carried to the Barley Mow where he died. The victor stood trial for murder but was later freed. This was the last recorded fatal duel in this country.

The Magna Carta monument.

> **REFRESHMENTS:**
> THE BARLEY MOW. An 18th century coaching inn pleasantly set overlooking the village green. Telephone: 01784 431857
> There are also tea rooms at one of the lodges on Runnymede (open daily, 8.30am to 5.30pm from April to September, 9.30am to 4.30pm from October to March).